JAZZ
BIBLE
SERIES
FAKE
BOOK

200 OF THE BEST SONGS FROM

RAGTIME
& EARLY JAZZ

Compiled and edited by Rob DuBoff

This series would not have been possible without encouragement from my family and friends. Thanks to: Grandma Lydia for helping me brainstorm for prospective titles, Mark Vinci and Mark Davis for sparking my interest in song collection, Jim and Jane Hall for their enthusiasm, Noel Silverman for being my advocate, Doug and Wendy for giving me perspective, and especially my parents, Arlene and Andy, for their tremendous support, confidence and guidance.

Special gratitude to Heather for being my sounding board, problem solver, editor, frequently-more-accurate extra set of ears and most importantly, my best friend. Without your unconditional support this project would not be.

THE JAZZ BIBLE™ and JAZZLINES PUBLICATIONS™ are trademarks used under license from Hero Enterprises, Inc.
Compiled and edited by Rob DuBoff for Jazzlines Publications™, a division of Hero Enterprises, Inc.

ISBN 0-7935-5806-9

HAL•LEONARD®
CORPORATION
7777 W. BLUEMOUND RD. P.O. BOX 13819 MILWAUKEE, WI 53213

200 OF THE BEST SONGS FROM
RAGTIME
& EARLY JAZZ
C O N T E N T S

4

FOREWORD

There are many publications called "fake books" in the music marketplace today. A fake book provides a collection of many standard and popular songs that are, in many cases, difficult to obtain. Unfortunately, fake books often utilize simplified or incorrect harmonies. When we are dealing with the music of many publishers over a period of a century, we often run into various differences in chord naming, notation and general editorial policy. Simply stated, many songs have come down to us with incorrect harmony and antiquated rhythmic notation. Often composers were consulted when their songs were prepared for sheet music editions, and a few even wrote their own piano/vocal arrangements for publication. But many established composers did not; so, many songs have been continuously available in arrangements that are not properly representative.

The idea of the 'standard classic song' is a relatively new one in American music. It was Frank Sinatra who popularized the performance of songs that were not current hit parade material, and even recorded them in 78 (and later 33 1/3) albums. In turn, jazz musicians and singers learned and collected the classic songs of Kern, Gershwin, Rodgers and Porter. Much of this repertoire was learned from recordings. The songs were often harmonically recomposed to make them more interesting for improvisation. In recent years, students seeking to learn these standards have similarly transcribed their favorite recordings. We felt that there should be a series of volumes containing the greatest popular songs with accurate melodies, chord progressions and lyrics. The Jazz Bible™ Series is the result.

The process for choosing titles to include was not complicated. A list of the 1000 most widely performed jazz standards was drafted, then evenly divided into five volumes, each representing a period of jazz. These volumes are:

RAGTIME AND EARLY JAZZ (1900-35)
THE SWING ERA (1936-47)
THE BEBOP ERA (1947-55)
JAZZ IN THE '50s (1950-59)
JAZZ IN THE '60s AND BEYOND (1960 - Present)

Generally, a song was placed in the era when it became popular, not necessarily when it was written. Unfortunately, several songs could not be included due to copyright restrictions.

Once the master title list was completed, the job of locating sources for each of the songs began. This proved to be a more complicated task than was first imagined. Songs were found in numerous libraries, such as The Library of Congress, The Smithsonian Archives, The Library of the Performing Arts at Lincoln Center, and many private collections throughout the United States. A number of these songs were quite rare, and some had to be assembled from scores or sketches. We then began listening to key recordings of these songs, with particular attention to classic jazz performances. (It was quite interesting to witness the metamorphosis of a song over many years of performances.) Through this research, we compiled the most commonly used chords for each song, many of which differed dramatically from the original sources. We refer to these substitute chords as the *adopted chord changes*. One of the difficulties in transcribing chord changes is distinguishing between harmonies that are commonly played and those that have been specifically arranged for a recording. To this end we have compared the adopted chord changes to the originals to ensure harmonic accuracy.

We have insured that this book be user-friendly by developing the following layout:

Generally, only one song is printed per page
A four-bar-to-a-line format has been used whenever possible
The form of each song can be seen at a glance with section
        marks that can also double as rehearsal letters

The volumes also include a chord glossary and biographies of many of the composers and lyricists.

CHORDS

There were many cases where we felt it was appropriate to include both the original and the adopted set of chords. The adopted chords appear in italics above the original chords. Where only italicized chords appear in any measure or an italicized chord with no other chord underneath, the original music had the previous chord continuing. In some cases the adopted chords clash with the melody; these instances are noted. We have also included turnaround chords at the end of every song; these are always italicized. A chord with the suffix *alt* implies that any altered chord can be substituted. (Please see the chord glossary for possible altered chords.)

FORM

The form of every song is clearly outlined with the use of section marks, each musically distinct section labeled a different letter. Where there is a section that is a variation of a preceding one, we have labeled the varying section with a superscript number. For example, A A^1 B A^2 would indicate that the form is A A B A with the second A varying slightly from the first A and the last A another variation. In cases where the verse to a song has been included, it is labeled V; an introduction is labeled I.

Naturally, each tune is open to difference in interpretation, and one should never rely solely on one source (be it printed or recorded) for learning songs. There is absolutely no substitute for developing one's ear through harmonic and melodic ear training, playing with others and listening to recordings.

We would be happy to hear your comments and criticisms, which will affect future editions in this series. An address is provided below.

Much research and thought went into the creation of this series, insuring that these fakebooks set new standards in printed music. They were undertaken with one thought in mind: you, the musician, should have the best possible printed sources for the finest songs of this century. I feel privileged to have been given the opportunity to work on this project. Thanks to Jim and Jane Hall, Noel Silverman, John Cerullo, Keith Mardak, and especially, Jeff Sultanof.

Robert DuBoff
C/O Hero Enterprises, Inc.
P.O. Box 1236
Saratoga Springs, NY 12866-0887

Please note that this is a **legal** fake book; **all fake books that do not display song copyright and ownership information somewhere on each title page are illegal.** Such publications violate U.S. intellectual property law by not reimbursing copyright owners for the use of their songs. Please help stop such infringements; do not buy these publications.

Rhythm Changes

(Based on the chord changes to "I Got Rhythm")

Blues Changes

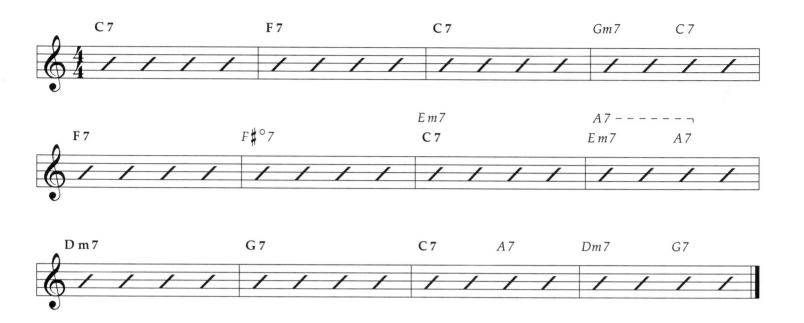

Minor Blues Changes

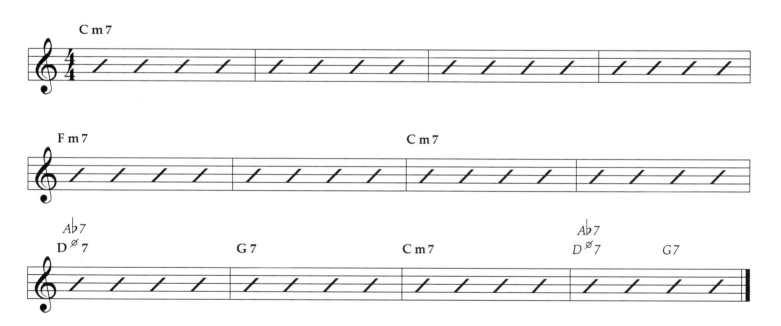

Chord Glossary

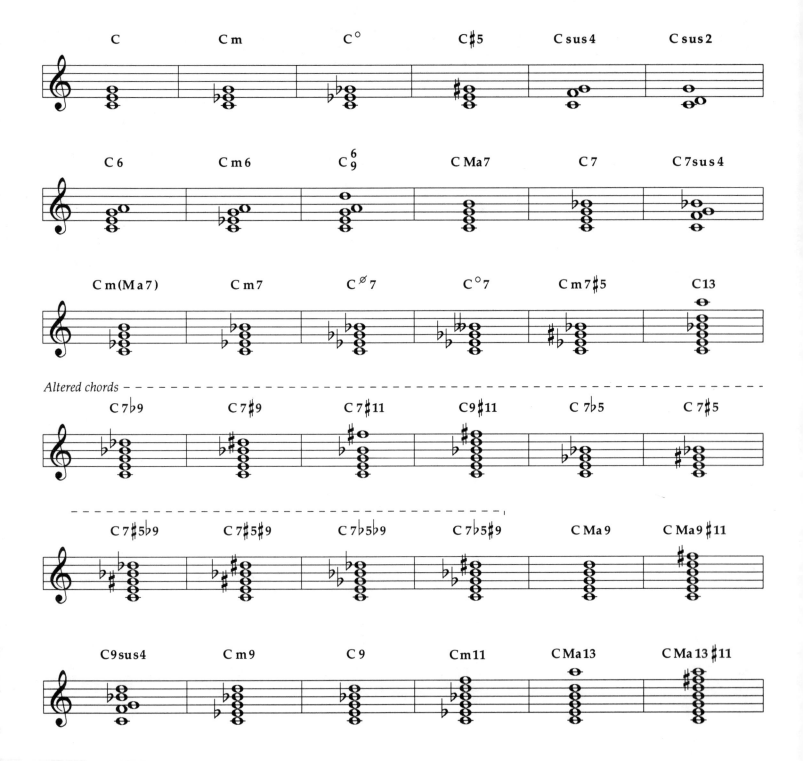

After You've Gone

Words by Henry Creamer
Music by Turner Layton

Ain't Misbehavin'

Words by Andy Razaf
Music by Thomas Waller and Harry Brooks

All of Me

Medium

Words and Music by Seymour Simons
and Gerald Marks

Always

Ballad or Medium

Words and Music by Irving Berlin

Note: This song was originally written in 3/4 time.

Amazing Grace

Words by John Newton
Traditional American Melody

Ballad

Among My Souvenirs

Medium

Words by Edgar Leslie
Music by Horatio Nicholls

Annie Doesn't Live Here Anymore

Words by Joe Young and Johnny Burke
Music by Harold Spina

As Long as I Live

Medium

Lyric by Ted Koehler
Music by Harold Arlen

Aunt Hagar's Blues

Medium

Words by J. Tim Brymn
Music by W.C. Handy

Old Dea-con Spliv-in', his flock was giv-in' the way of liv-in' right,

said he "No wing-in', no rag-time sing-in' to-night."

Up jumped Aunt Ha-gar, and shout-ed out with all her might:

Oh, 'taint no use o' preach-in', oh, 'taint no use o' teach-in',

each mod-u-la-tion of syn-co-pa-tion just tells my feet to dance and I can't re-fuse

when I hear the mel-o-dy they call the blues; those ev-er lov-in' blues. Just

hear Aunt Ha-gar's chil-dren har-mon-iz-in' to that old mourn-ful tune, it's

like a choir from on high broke loose. If the

deb-bil brought it the good Lawd sent it right down to me, let the

con-gre-ga-tion join while I sing those lov-in' Aunt Ha-gar's blues.

Autumn in New York

Ballad

Words and Music by Vernon Duke

Avalon

Medium

Words by Al Jolson and B.G. DeSylva
Music by Vincent Rose

Basin Street Blues

Medium

Words and Music by Spencer Williams

Note: Substitute lyrics are in italics.

Battle Hymn of the Republic

Medium

Words by Julia Ward Howe
Music by William Steffe

The Best Things in Life Are Free

Medium

Music and Lyrics by B.G. DeSylva,
Lew Brown and Ray Henderson

The Birth of the Blues

Medium

Words by B.G. DeSylva and Lew Brown
Music by Ray Henderson

Black and Tan Fantasy

Medium

By Duke Ellington
and Bub Miley

Note: For solos use standard blues changes in B flat (See "Blues Changes").

Blame It on My Youth

Ballad

Words by Edward Heyman
Music by Oscar Levant

The Blue Room

Medium

Words by Lorenz Hart
Music by Richard Rodgers

Blue Skies

Medium

Words and Music by Irving Berlin

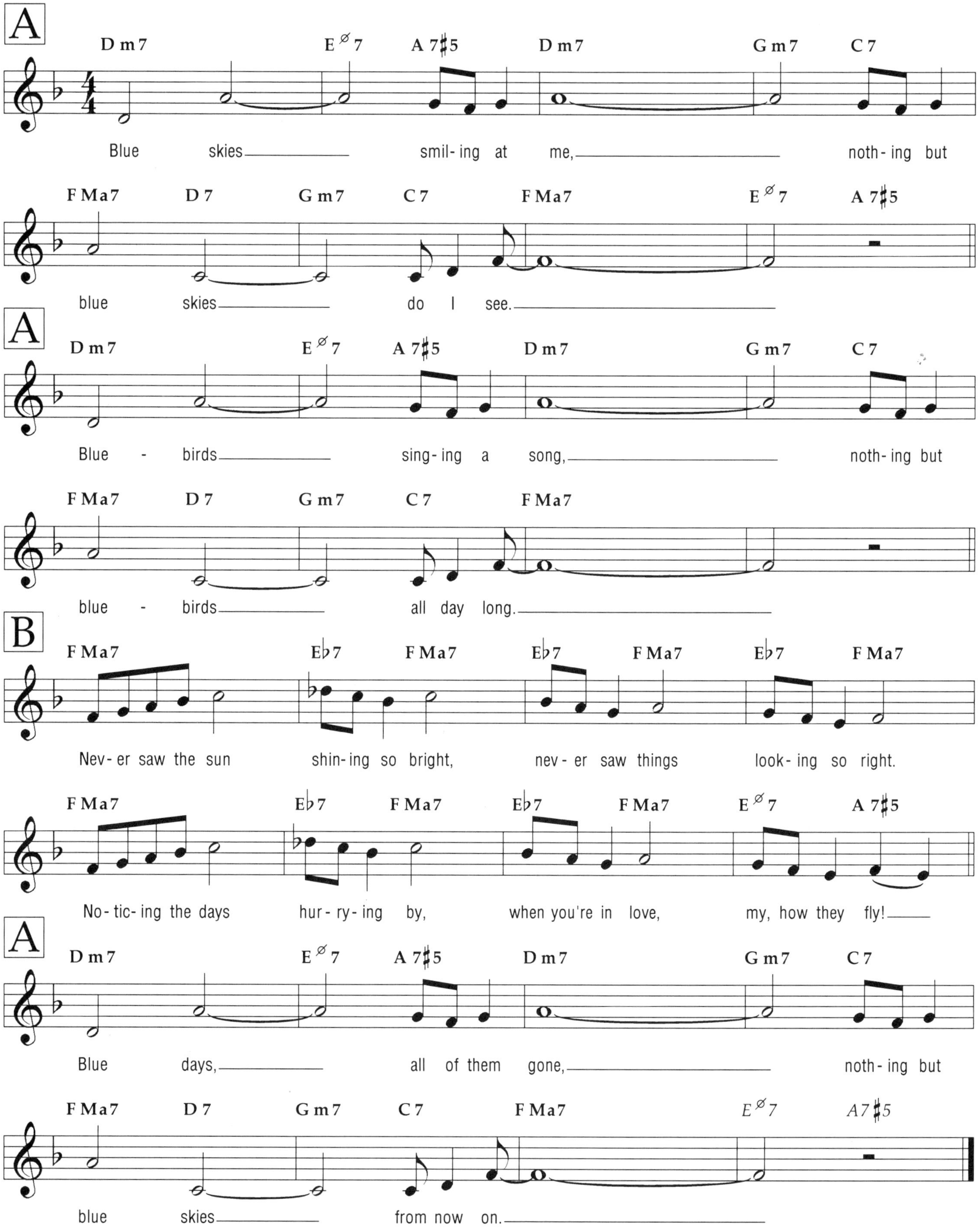

Body and Soul

Bugle Call Rag

By Jack Pettis,
Billy Meyers and Elmer Schoebel

Bye Bye Blackbird

Lyric by Mort Dixon
Music by Ray Henderson

Medium

Bye Bye Blues

Medium

Words and Music by Fred Hamm, Dave Bennett,
Bert Lown and Chauncey Gray

Can't Help Lovin' Dat Man

Ballad or Medium

Lyrics by Oscar Hammerstein II
Music by Jerome Kern

Cocktails for Two

Medium

Words and Music by Arthur Johnston
and Sam Coslow

Copenhagen

Medium

Lyric by Walter Melrose
Music by Charlie Davis

Note: Use the italicized turnaround
chords in measure 8 the first time only.

Dancing on the Ceiling

Words by Lorenz Hart
Music by Richard Rodgers

Medium

Danny Boy
(Londonderry Air)

Words by Frederick Edward Weatherly
Music is Irish Traditional

Dardanella

Medium

Words by Fred Fisher
Music by Felix Bernard and Johnny S. Black

Dinah

Medium

Words by Sam M. Lewis and Joe Young
Music by Harry Akst

Do I Love You

Ballad

Lyrics by Leo Robin
Music by Ralph Rainger

Do You Know What It Means to Miss New Orleans

Lyric by Eddie De Lange
Music by Louis Alter

Ballad

Don't Be That Way

Medium

By Benny Goodman
Mitchell Parish and Edgar Sampson

Don't Worry 'Bout Me

Ballad

Lyric by Ted Koehler
Music by Rube Bloom

Down by the River

Ballad

Words by Lorenz Hart
Music by Richard Rodgers

Dream a Little Dream of Me

Words by Gus Kahn
Music by Wilbur Schwandt and Fabian Andree

Drop Me Off in Harlem

Medium

Words by Nick Kenny
Music by Duke Ellington

East of the Sun
(And West of the Moon)

Words and Music by Brooks Bowman

Everybody Loves My Baby
(But My Baby Don't Love Nobody but Me)

Medium

Words and Music by Jack Palmer
and Spencer Williams

Everything I Have Is Yours

Ballad

Words by Harold Adamson
Music by Burton Lane

Exactly Like You

Medium

Words by Dorothy Fields
Music by Jimmy McHugh

Falling in Love with Love

Medium

Words by Lorenz Hart
Music by Richard Rodgers

Fascination
(Valse Tzigane)

Ballad

By F.D. Marchetti

Five Foot Two, Eyes of Blue

(Has Anybody Seen My Girl?)

Medium

Words by Joe Young and Sam Lewis
Music by Ray Henderson

For All We Know

Medium

Words by Sam M. Lewis
Music by J. Fred Coots

Gee Baby, Ain't I Good to You

Ballad

Words by Don Redman and Andy Razaf
Music by Don Redman

Get Happy

Bright

Lyric by Ted Koehler
Music by Harold Arlen

* Often the melody and chords for this
measure are incorrectly lowered a half step.

The Glory of Love

Medium

Words and Music by Billy Hill

Hallelujah

Bright

Words by Clifford Grey and Leo Robin
Music by Vincent Youmans

Have You Met Miss Jones?

Medium

Words by Lorenz Hart
Music by Richard Rodgers

62

Here in My Arms

Medium

Words by Lorenz Hart
Music by Richard Rodgers

Honeysuckle Rose

Medium

Words by Andy Razaf
Music by Thomas "Fats" Waller

How About Me?

Ballad

Words and Music by Irving Berlin

A

E♭Ma7   A♭7   D♭Ma7   Gø7   C7♯5

It's o - ver, all o - ver, and soon some - bod - y else___ will

Fm   Fm(Ma7)   Fm7   B♭7   Gm7   C7   Fm7   B♭7

make a fuss___ a - bout you, but how___ a - bout me?___

A¹

E♭Ma7   A♭7   D♭Ma7   Gø7   C7♯5

It's o - ver, all o - ver, and soon some - bod - y else___ will

Fm   Fm(Ma7)   Fm7   B♭7   E♭Ma7   A♭7   E♭Ma7   G7♯5

tell his friends___ a - bout you, but how___ a - bout me?___ You'll find some -

B

A♭Ma7   Aø7   D7   Gm7   C7

bod - y new,___ but what am I to do?___ I'll still re -

Fm7   Cm7   F7   Fm7   B♭7

mem - ber you___ when you___ have for - got - ten.

A¹

E♭Ma7   A♭7   D♭Ma7   Gø7   C7♯5

And may - be a ba - by will climb up - on your knee___ and

Fm   Fm(Ma7)   Fm7   B♭7   E♭Ma7   *Fm7*   *B♭7*

put it's arms___ a - bout you, but how___ a - bout me?___

How Deep Is the Ocean

(How High Is the Sky)

Ballad

Words and Music by Irving Berlin

I Can Dream, Can't I?

Ballad

Lyric by Irving Kahal
Music by Sammy Fain

I Can't Believe That You're in Love with Me

Medium

Words and Music by Jimmy McHugh
and Clarence Gaskill

I Can't Give You Anything but Love

Medium

Words by Dorothy Fields
Music by Jimmy McHugh

I Cried for You

Words and Music by Arthur Freed,
Gus Arnheim and Abe Lyman

I Don't Stand a Ghost of a Chance

Ballad

Words by Bing Crosby and Ned Washington
Music by Victor Young

I Never Knew

Medium

Words and Music by Gus Kahn
and Ted Fiorito

I Won't Dance

Lyrics by Oscar Hammerstein and Otto Harbach
Screen Version by Dorothy Fields and Jimmy McHugh
Music by Jerome Kern

73

I Wished on the Moon

Medium

Words and Music by Dorothy Parker
and Ralph Rainger

I'll Get By

(As Long as I Have You)

Medium

Lyric by Roy Turk
Music by Fred E. Ahlert

I'm a Dreamer, Aren't We All

Medium

Words and Music by B.G. DeSylva,
Lew Brown and Ray Henderson

I'm Always Chasing Rainbows

Medium

Words by Joseph McCarthy
Music by Harry Carroll

I'm Confessin'
(That I Love You)

Medium

Words and Music by Al Neiberg,
Doc Daugherty and Ellis Reynolds

I'm Putting All My Eggs in One Basket

Medium

Words and Music by Irving Berlin

I'm Sitting on Top of the World

Medium

Words by Sam M. Lewis and Joe Young
Music by Ray Henderson

I'm Yours

Medium

Words by E.Y. Harburg
Music by Johnny Green

I've Got a Feeling I'm Falling

Medium

Words and Music by Harry Link,
Billy Rose and Thomas "Fats" Waller

I've Got the World on a String

Medium

Lyric by Ted Koehler
Music by Harold Arlen

I've Told Ev'ry Little Star

Bright

Lyrics by Oscar Hammerstein II
Music by Jerome Kern

Ill Wind
(You're Blowin' Me No Good)

Lyric by Ted Koehler
Music by Harold Arlen

Medium

In a Little Spanish Town

('Twas on a Night Like This)

Words by Sam M. Lewis and Joe Young
Music by Mabel Wayne

Ballad

In a Shanty in Old Shanty Town

Medium

Words by Joe Young
Music by Little Jack Little and John Siras

Indiana
(Back Home Again in Indiana)

Words by Ballard MacDonald
Music by James F. Hanley

Bright

Isn't It Romantic?

Words by Lorenz Hart
Music by Richard Rodgers

Medium

It All Depends on You

Medium

Words and Music by B.G. DeSylva,
Lew Brown and Ray Henderson

It Don't Mean a Thing
(If It Ain't Got That Swing)

Words and Music by Duke Ellington
and Irving Mills

It's Easy to Remember

Words by Lorenz Hart
Music by Richard Rodgers

Ballad

It's the Talk of the Town

Ballad or Medium

Words by Marty Symes and Al Neiburg
Music by Jerry Livingston

94

Ja-Da

Medium

Words and Music by Bob Carleton

Copyright © 1996 HAL LEONARD CORPORATION
International Copyright Secured   All Rights Reserved

The Joint Is Jumpin'

Medium

Words by Andy Razaf and J.C. Johnson
Music by Thomas "Fats" Waller

Just a Gigolo

Original German Text by Julius Brammer
English Words by Irving Caesar
Music by Leonello Casucci

Medium

Just Imagine

Medium

Words and Music by B.G. DeSylva,
Lew Brown and Ray Henderson

Just One More Chance

Medium

Words by Sam Coslow
Music by Arthur Johnston

Last Night When We Were Young

Ballad

Lyric by E.Y. Harburg
Music by Harold Arlen

Let's Dance

Words by Fanny Baldridge
Music by Gregory Stone and Joseph Bonine

Medium

Let's Fall in Love

Medium

Words by Ted Koehler
Music by Harold Arlen

A

EbMa7 Cm7 Fm7 Bb7 EbMa7 Cm7 Fm7 Bb7

Let's fall in love, why should-n't we____ fall in love? Our hearts are made____

Gm7 Cm7 Fm7 Bb7 Gm7 C7 Fm7 Bb7

____ of it, let's take a chance,____ why be a-fraid____ of it?____

A

EbMa7 Cm7 Fm7 Bb7 EbMa7 Cm7 Fm7 Bb7

Let's close our eyes, and make our own____ par - a - dise. Lit - tle we know____

Gm7 Cm7 Fm7 Bb7 D∅7 G7#5

____ of it, still we can try____ to make a go____ of it.____

B

Cm7 3 F7

We might have been meant for each oth - er.____ To

BbMa7 A∅7 3 D7#5 Gm7 C7b9 Fm7 Bb7

be or not to be, let our hearts dis - cov - er.

A¹

EbMa7 Cm7 Fm7 Bb7 EbMa7 Cm7 Fm7 Bb7

Let's fall in love, why should-n't we____ fall in love? Now is the time____

Gm7 Cm7 3 Fm7 Bb7 EbMa7 Cm7 Fm7 Bb7

____ for it while we are young, let's fall in love.____

Little Girl Blue

Words by Lorenz Hart
Music by Richard Rodgers

Little Man You've Had a Busy Day

Ballad

Words by Maurice Sigler and Al Hoffman
Music by Mabel Wayne

Little White Lies

Medium

Words and Music by Walter Donaldson

Loch Lomond

Medium

Traditional

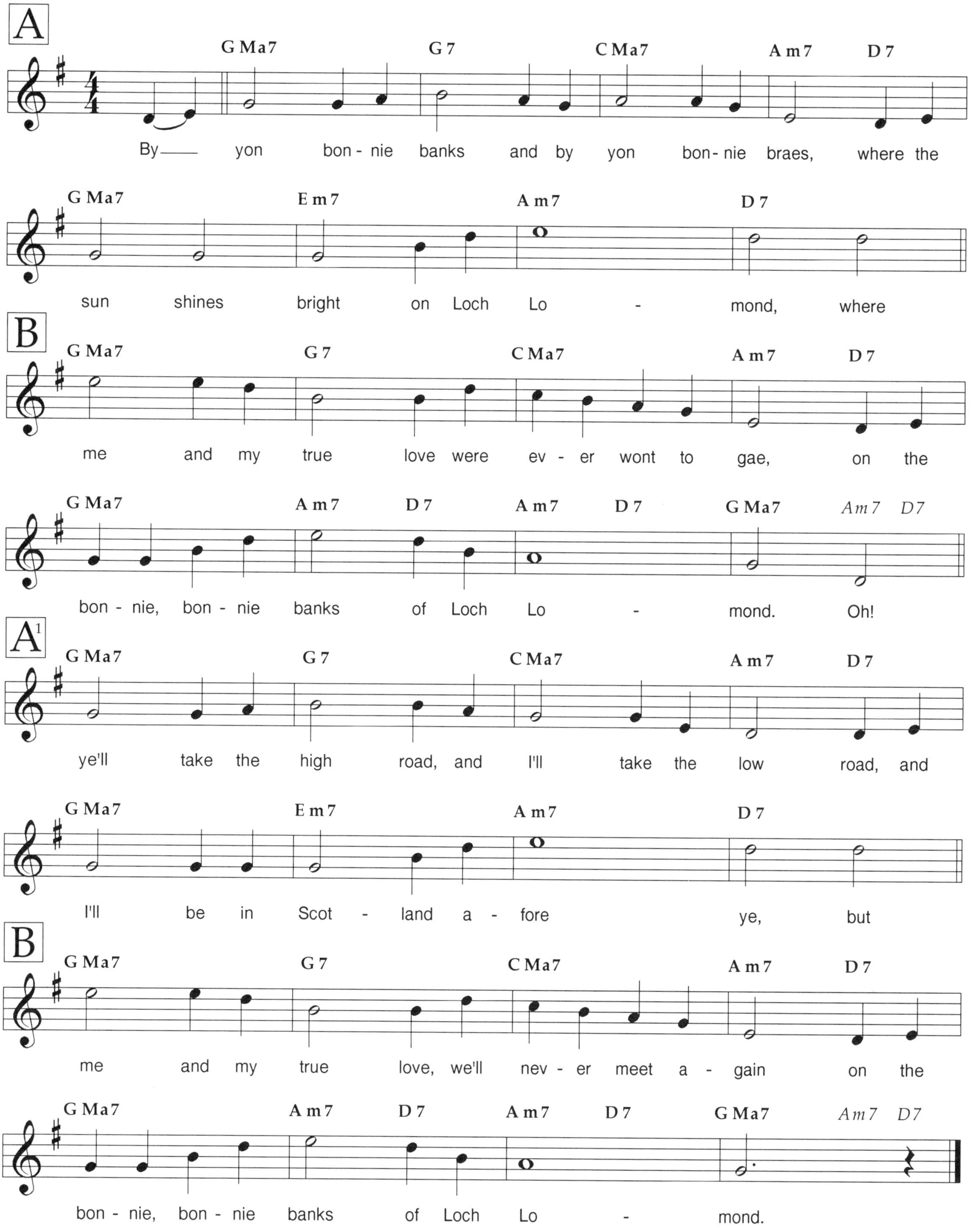

A
GMa7 G7 CMa7 Am7 D7
By yon bon-nie banks and by yon bon-nie braes, where the
GMa7 Em7 Am7 D7
sun shines bright on Loch Lo - mond, where
B
GMa7 G7 CMa7 Am7 D7
me and my true love were ev - er wont to gae, on the
GMa7 Am7 D7 Am7 D7 GMa7 Am7 D7
bon - nie, bon - nie banks of Loch Lo - mond. Oh!
A1
GMa7 G7 CMa7 Am7 D7
ye'll take the high road, and I'll take the low road, and
GMa7 Em7 Am7 D7
I'll be in Scot - land a - fore ye, but
B
GMa7 G7 CMa7 Am7 D7
me and my true love, we'll nev - er meet a - gain on the
GMa7 Am7 D7 Am7 D7 GMa7 Am7 D7
bon - nie, bon - nie banks of Loch Lo - mond.

The Lonesome Road

Words by Gene Austin
Music by Nathaniel Shilkret

Look for the Silver Lining

Medium

Words by Buddy DeSylva
Music by Jerome Kern

Love Is Just around the Corner

Medium

Words and Music by Leo Robin
and Lewis E. Gensler

Love Me or Leave Me

Medium

Lyrics by Gus Kahn
Music by Walter Donaldson

Lover

Words by Lorenz Hart
Music by Richard Rodgers

Note: This song was originally written in 3/4 time.

Lover, Come Back to Me

Bright

Lyrics by Oscar Hammerstein II
Music by Sigmund Romberg

Lullaby of the Leaves

Medium

Words by Joe Young
Music by Bernice Petkere

Mad about the Boy

Medium

Words and Music by Noel Coward

Makin' Whoopee!

Medium

Lyrics by Gus Kahn
Music by Walter Donaldson

Margie

Medium

Words by Benny Davis
Music by Con Conrad and J. Russell Robinson

Mean to Me

Medium

Lyric and Music by Fred E. Ahlert
and Roy Turk

Memories of You

Lyric by Andy Razaf
Music by Eubie Blake

Medium

Milenberg Joys

Words by Walter Melrose
Music by Leon Roppolo,
Paul Mares and Ferdinand "Jelly Roll" Morton

Miss Brown to You

Medium

By Leo Robin,
Richard A. Whiting and Ralph Rainger

Mood Indigo

Ballad

Words and Music by Duke Ellington,
Irving Mills and Albany Bigard

Moon Song

Medium

Words by Sam Coslow
Music by Arthur Johnston

Moonglow

Medium

Words and Music by Will Hudson,
Eddie De Lange and Irving Mills

Moonlight Bay

Ballad

Words by Edward Madden
Music by Percy Wenrich

Moonlight on the Ganges

Medium

Lyric by Chester Wallace
Music by Sherman Myers

More than You Know

Ballad

Words by William Rose and Edward Eliscu
Music by Vincent Youmans

Moten Swing

Medium

By Buster Moten
and Bennie Moten

My Blue Heaven

Medium

Lyric by George Whiting
Music by Walter Donaldson

My Heart Stood Still

Medium

Words by Lorenz Hart
Music by Richard Rodgers

My Ideal

Words by Leo Robin
Music by Richard A. Whiting and Newell Chase

Ballad

will I pass him by and nev- er e- ven know that he is my i - deal?

My Kinda Love

Medium

Lyrics by Jo Trent
Music by Louis Alter

My Melancholy Baby

Medium

Words by George Norton
Music by Ernie Burnett

My Old Flame

Ballad

Words and Music by Arthur Johnston
and Sam Coslow

Nevertheless
(I'm in Love with You)

Words and Music by Bert Kalmar
and Harry Ruby

Ballad

The Night Is Young
(And You're So Beautiful)

Words by Billy Rose and Irving Kahal
Music by Dana Suesse

Ballad

Nobody Knows the Trouble I've Seen

Traditional Spiritual

Medium

Oh, no-bod - y knows the trou - ble I've seen, no-bod - y knows but Je - sus! No-bod - y knows the trou - ble I've seen, glo - ry, hal - le - lu - jah!

Ol' Man River

Medium

Lyrics by Oscar Hammerstein II
Music by Jerome Kern

Oh! You Beautiful Doll

Medium

Words by A. Seymour Brown
Music by Nat D. Ayer

On the Sunny Side of the Street

Medium

Lyric by Dorothy Fields
Music by Jimmy McHugh

Out of Nowhere

Medium

Words by Edward Heyman
Music by Johnny Green

Penthouse Serenade

Medium

Words and Music by Will Jason
and Val Burton

Please

Words by Leo Robin
Music by Ralph Rainger

Medium

Poor Butterfly

Medium

Words by John L. Golden
Music by Raymond Hubbell

Prisoner of Love

Medium

Words and Music by Leo Robin,
Clarence Gaskill and Russ Columbo

Puttin' on the Ritz

Medium

Words and Music by Irving Berlin

Remember

Medium

Words and Music by Irving Berlin

Note: This song is also commonly played in 4/4 time.

Ring Dem Bells

Medium

Words and Music by Duke Ellington
and Irving Mills

Rockin' Chair

Medium

Words and Music by Hoagy Carmichael

Old rock-in' chair's got me,——— cane by my side;

fetch me that gin, son, 'fore I tan your hide.

Can't get from this ca-bin,——— goin' no-where;

just sit me here grab-bin' at the flies 'round this rock-in' chair.

My dear old Aunt Har-ri-et, in heav-en she be,

sent me sweet cha-ri-ot——— for the end of these trou-ble I see.

Old rock-in' chair gits it,——— judge-ment day is here,

chained to my rock-in' chair.———

Copyright © 1929, 1930 Hoagy Publishing Company
Copyrights Renewed 1957, 1958
Administered by All Nations Music
International Copyright Secured   All Rights Reserved

Rose of Washington Square

Medium

Lyric by Ballard MacDonald
Music by James F. Hanley

Rose Room

Medium

Words by Harry Williams
Music by Art Hickman

Roses of Picardy

Medium

Words by Fred E. Weatherly
Music by Haydn Wood

Royal Garden Blues

Medium

Words and Music by Clarence Williams
and Spencer Williams

Rosetta

Medium

Words and Music by Earl Hines
and Henri Wood

San

Medium

Words and Music by Lindsay McPhail
and Walter Michels

Say It Isn't So

Medium

Words and Music by Irving Berlin

Say it is - n't so,_____ say it is - n't so._____

Ev - 'ry-one is say - ing you don't love me, say it is - n't so._____

Ev - 'ry-where I go,_____ ev - 'ry-one I know_____

whis- pers that you're grow-ing tired____ of me, say it is - n't so._____

Peo - ple say that you_____ found some- bod - y new,_____

and it won't be long be - fore you leave me, say it is - n't true._____

Say that ev - 'ry-thing is still o - kay, that's all I want to know,_____ and what they're

say - ing,_____ say it is - n't so._____

September Song

Ballad

Words by Maxwell Anderson
Music by Kurt Weill

She's Funny That Way

Medium

Words by Richard A. Whiting
Music by Neil Moret

Sheik of Araby

Bright

Words by Harry B. Smith and Francis Wheeler
Music by Ted Snyder

Shine

Medium

Words by Cecil Mack and Lew Brown
Music by Ford Dabney

A Ship without a Sail

Words by Lorenz Hart
Music by Richard Rodgers

Ballad

Singin' the Blues till My Daddy Comes Home

Medium

Lyric by Sam M. Lewis and Joe Young
Music by Con Conrad and J. Russell Robinson

Smoke Gets in Your Eyes

Ballad

Words by Otto Harbach
Music by Jerome Kern

Smoke Rings

Medium

Words by Ned Washington
Music by H. Eugene Gifford

Blow, blow them ev - 'ry - where, give your trou - bles wings.

A¹

What do they tell____ and what is the spell____ they cast?____

Some of them fall____ and seem to re - call____ the past.____ But

most of them rise____ a - way to the skies____ of blue.____ Oh, lit - tle

smoke rings I love,____ please take me a - bove,____ take me with you!____

Softly as in a Morning Sunrise

Medium

Lyric by Oscar Hammerstein II
Music by Sigmund Romberg

Solitude

Ballad

Words and Music by Duke Ellington,
Eddie De Lange and Irving Mills

Some of These Days

Medium

Words and Music by Shelton Brooks

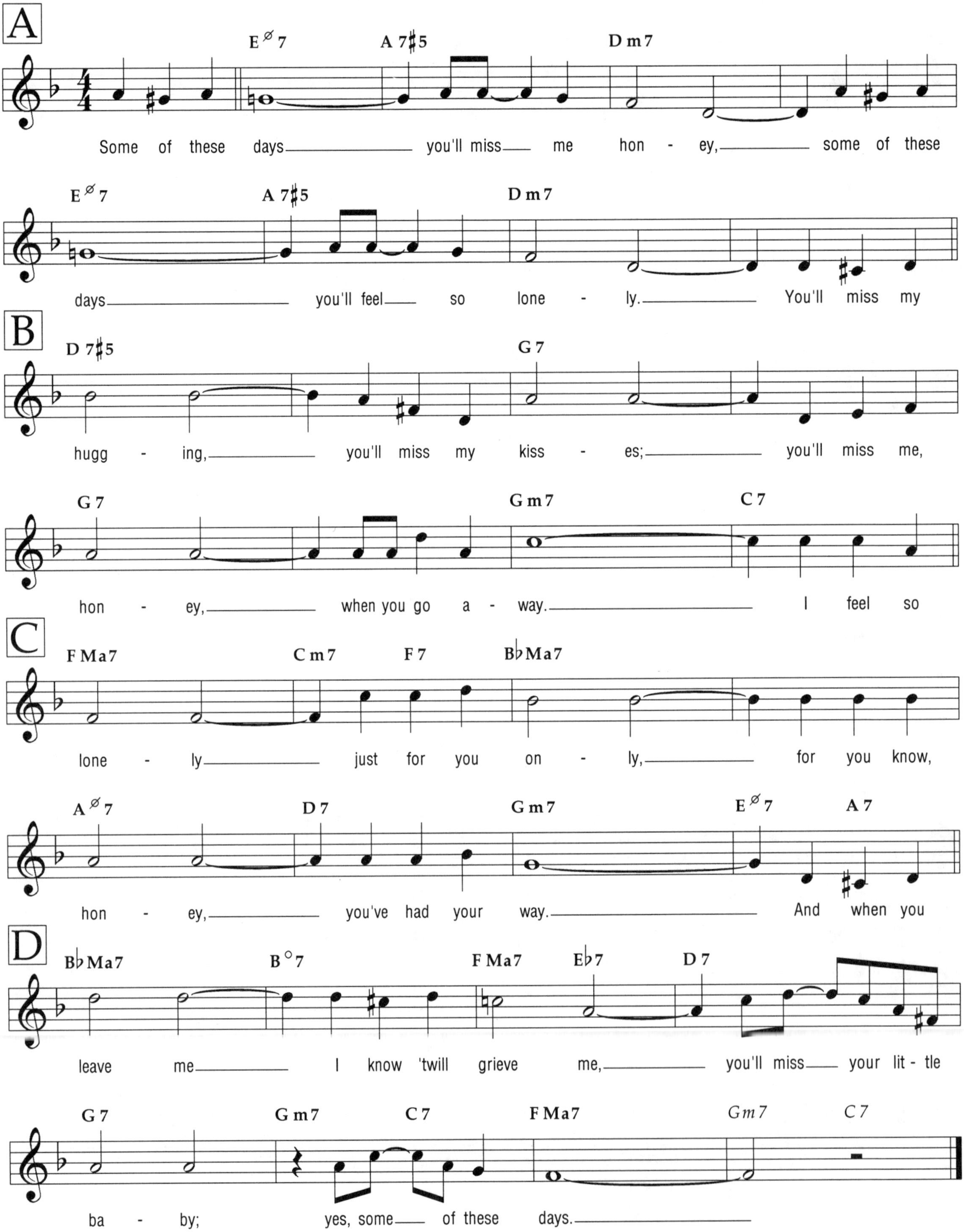

A
E∅7 A7♯5 Dm7
Some of these days you'll miss me hon - ey, some of these
E∅7 A7♯5 Dm7
days you'll feel so lone - ly. You'll miss my
B
D7♯5 G7
hugg - ing, you'll miss my kiss - es; you'll miss me,
G7 Gm7 C7
hon - ey, when you go a - way. I feel so
C
FMa7 Cm7 F7 B♭Ma7
lone - ly just for you on - ly, for you know,
A∅7 D7 Gm7 E∅7 A7
hon - ey, you've had your way. And when you
D
B♭Ma7 B°7 FMa7 E♭7 D7
leave me I know 'twill grieve me, you'll miss your lit - tle
G7 Gm7 C7 FMa7 Gm7 C7
ba - by; yes, some of these days.

Somebody Loves Me

Medium

Words by B.G. DeSylva and Ballard MacDonald
Music by George Gershwin
French Version by Emelia Renaud

Someday I'll Find You

Medium

Words and Music by Noel Coward

Sometimes I'm Happy

Medium

Words by Clifford Grey and Irving Caesar
Music by Vincent Youmans

The Song Is You

Bright

Lyrics by Oscar Hammerstein II
Music by Jerome Kern

Song of the Islands

Ballad

Words and Music by Charles E. King

Sophisticated Lady

Ballad

Words and Music by Duke Ellington,
Irving Mills and Mitchell Parish

St. Louis Blues

Ballad or Medium

By W.C. Handy

Squeeze Me

Medium

Words and Music by Clarence Williams
and Thomas Waller

Star Dust

Ballad

Words by Mitchell Parish
Music by Hoagy Carmichael

* Note: Both of these two chords are commonly played. B7 is more common.

Stay as Sweet as You Are

Medium

Words by Mack Gordon
Music by Harry Revel

Sugar

Words by Joe Young
Music by George Meyer

Medium

Sweet Sue-Just You

Medium

Words by Will J. Harris
Music by Victor Young

Thanks

Words by Sam Coslow
Music by Arthur Johnston

Medium

There'll Be Some Changes Made

Words by Billy Higgins
Music by W. Benton Overstreet

Medium

They Didn't Believe Me

Ballad

Words by Herbert Reynolds
Music by Jerome Kern

Thou Swell

Medium

Words by Lorenz Hart
Music by Richard Rodgers

The Thrill Is Gone

Words by Lew Brown
Music by Ray Henderson

Ballad

Tiger Rag
(Hold That Tiger)

Words by Harry DeCosta
Music by Original Dixieland Jazz Band

The Touch of Your Lips

Ballad

Words and Music by Ray Noble

Under a Blanket of Blue

Medium

Words by Marty Symes and Al J. Neiburg
Music by Jerry Livingston

Walkin' My Baby Back Home

Ballad

Words and Music by Roy Turk
and Fred E. Ahlert

The Way You Look Tonight

Medium

Words by Dorothy Fields
Music by Jerome Kern

Note: Take the coda the last time.

What Is There to Say

Ballad

Words and Music by Vernon Duke
and E.Y. Harburg

What'll I Do?

Ballad

Words and Music by Irving Berlin

A

3/4

C Ma7　　F m 7　Bb 7　C Ma7　　F m 7　Bb 7

What-'ll I do_____ when you_____ are far_____ a - way_____ and

Em7
C Ma7　　A 7　D m7　G 7　C Ma7　　D m7　G 7

I_____ am blue, what-'ll I do?_____ What-'ll I

A

C Ma7　　F m 7　Bb 7　C Ma7　　F m 7　Bb 7

do_____ when I_____ am won - d'ring who_____ is

Em7
C Ma7　　A 7　D m7　G 7　C Ma7　　G m7　C 7

kiss - ing you, what-'ll I do?_____ What-'ll I

B

F Ma7　　G m7　C 7　F Ma7　　Bb 7

do_____ with just_____ a pho - to-graph_____ to

E m7　　A 7　D 7　D m7　G 7

tell_____ my trou - bles to?_____ When I'm a-

A

C Ma7　　F m 7　Bb 7　C Ma7　　F m 7　Bb 7

lone_____ with on - ly dreams_____ of you_____ that

Em7
C Ma7　　A 7　D m7　G 7　C Ma7　　Dm 7　G 7

won't_____ come true, what-'ll I do?_____

© Copyright 1924 by Irving Berlin
© Arrangement Copyright 1947 by Irving Berlin
Copyright Renewed
International Copyright Secured   All Rights Reserved

When I Take My Sugar to Tea

Medium

Words and Music by Sammy Fain,
Irving Kahal and Pierre Norman

When Lights Are Low

Medium

Words by Spencer Williams
Music by Benny Carter

When My Baby Smiles at Me

Medium

Words and Music by Harry Von Tilzer,
Andrew B. Sterling, Bill Munro and Ted Lewis

When You and I Were Young, Maggie

Medium

Words by George W. Johnson
Music by James Austin Butterfield

Where the Blue of the Night
(Meets the Gold of the Day)

Medium

Lyric and Music by Fred E. Ahlert,
Bing Crosby and Roy Turk

Whispering

Medium

Words and Music by Richard Coburn,
John Schonberger and Vincent Rose

Why Do I Love You?

Medium

Lyrics by Oscar Hammerstein II
Music by Jerome Kern

Why Was I Born?

Medium

Lyrics by Oscar Hammerstein II
Music by Jerome Kern

Without a Song

Bright

Words by William Rose and Edward Eliscu
Music by Vincent Youmans

Note: In this arrangement, all rhythmic values in the A Sections have been doubled
from how they appeared in the original music (the "Bridge" or B Section has remained the same).
In addition, those sections have been increased from 8 to 16 bars in length.
This is the most common arrangement of this song.

With a Song in My Heart

Medium

Words by Lorenz Hart
Music by Richard Rodgers

The World Is Waiting for the Sunrise

Words by Eugene Lockhart
Music by Ernest Seitz

Ballad

Note: When this song is played at medium or
bright tempos, all rhythmic values are doubled.

Wrap Your Troubles in Dreams

(And Dream Your Troubles Away)

Lyric by Ted Koehler and Billy Moll
Music by Harry Barris

Medium

Yesterdays

Words by Otto Harbach
Music by Jerome Kern

Medium

You Are Too Beautiful

Ballad

Words by Lorenz Hart
Music by Richard Rodgers

You Brought a New Kind of Love to Me

Medium

Words and Music by Sammy Fain,
Irving Kahal and Pierre Norman

You Call It Madness
(But I Call It Love)

Medium

Words and Music by Con Conrad,
Gladys DuBois, Russ Columbo and Paul Gregory

You Hit the Spot

Medium

Words and Music by Mack Gordon
and Harry Revel

You Made Me Love You

(I Didn't Want to Do It)

Words by Joe McCarthy
Music by James V. Monaco

Medium

You Took Advantage of Me

Medium

Words by Lorenz Hart
Music by Richard Rodgers

You're Driving Me Crazy!

(What Did I Do?)

Words and Music by Walter Donaldson

Medium

You're Mine, You!

Ballad or Medium

Words by Edward Heyman
Music by Johnny Green

You're My Everything

Medium

Lyric by Mort Dixon and Joe Young
Music by Harry Warren

You're the Cream in My Coffee

Medium

Words and Music by B.G. DeSylva,
Lew Brown and Ray Henderson

200 OF THE BEST SONGS FROM

RAGTIME

BIOGRAPHIES

& EARLY JAZZ

HOAGY CARMICHAEL

The composer of many jazz-tinged standards, Hoagland Carmichael was born in Bloomington, Indiana in 1899. He studied piano with his mother, a pianist in motion picture houses. He was leading bands and playing for dances while still in high school. He attended Indiana University with the intention of becoming a lawyer, but his friendship with cornetist Bix Beiderbecke resulted in Hoagy's composing music for Bix's band. Hoagy's composition "Riverboat Shuffle" was even recorded by Bix (and when Bix joined the Paul Whiteman orchestra, Whiteman recorded it with Hoagy singing and playing piano).

When Hoagy wrote "Star Dust" in 1927, he was still concentrating on his law studies. But by 1929, he'd moved to New York to become a professional songwriter. "Star Dust" was recorded by Isham Jones' orchestra and became a smash hit; one of the most frequently recorded songs in American music. Hoagy later wrote and recorded "Rockin' Chair," "Georgia On My Mind," "Lazy River" and "Lazybones," all of them big hits.

He went out to Hollywood to write for motion pictures, and the songs "Moonburn," "Small Fry" and "Two Sleepy People" resulted. In 1937, he took his first acting job in films; he would appear in several motion pictures, including "To Have And Have Not," "The Best Years Of Our Lives" and "Young Man With A Horn." Carmichael continued to produce many song hits in the 40s and 50s, among them "The Nearness Of You," "Skylark," "Memphis In June," "Baltimore Oriole," "How Little We Know" and "In The Cool, Cool, Cool Of The Evening," which won the Academy Award for best song in 1950. He went into retirement in the 60s, playing golf and recording occasionally. He died in Palm Springs, California in 1981.

SAM COSLOW

Coslow had an amazingly varied career: songwriter, singer, vaudevillian, motion picture producer, and even founder/publisher of a Wall Street service publication "Indicator Digest".

He was born in New York in 1902 and was a published composer while still in his teens. During those years, he also contributed a column to Variety magazine, and even served as a music adviser to Edison Records. He wrote a number of successful songs in the 20s, and received a big break when Eddie Cantor sang his song "Bebe;" Cantor subsequently arranged for Coslow to write special material for the Ziegfeld Follies.

Coslow and Larry Spier started their own publishing company in 1927; the company was bought in 1929 by Paramount and later renamed Famous Music Company. Coslow became a staff songwriter for Paramount, and the songs "Sing, You Sinners," "Thanks," "Just One More Chance," "My Old Flame," "Learn To Croon" and "The Day You Came Along" resulted. With his frequent collaborator Arthur Johnston, he wrote perhaps his biggest hit, "Cocktails For Two" for singer Carl Brisson.

In the early 40s, Coslow was a partner in the Soundies Corporation, the legendary company that produced short video presentations of song hits that were played on video juke boxes; the juke boxes were quite popular at hotels and bars for a number of years. Coslow returned to Paramount in the mid 40s to produce motion pictures.

By the end of the 50s, Coslow devoted his time to his stock investments. In 1974, he was elected into the The Songwriter's Hall Of Fame. He died in New York in 1982.

NOEL COWARD

Coward distinguished himself as an actor, writer, director, songwriter and producer in Britain and the United States. He was born in Teddington, Middlesex, England in 1899, and played his first part on the stage in 1911. The first song in which he wrote both words and music was "Forbidden Fruit" in 1916, and his first solo play, Rat Trap, was produced in 1918. In the 20s, he was writing several plays and sketches for the British stage, and appeared in many of them as an actor-singer.

He wrote the first of his many songs for his lifelong friend Gertrude Lawrence in 1923, "Parisian Pierrot." His other songwriting successes were "Poor Little Rich Girl," "Bittersweet," "I'll See You Again," "Ziguener," "Mad Dogs And Englishmen," "A Room With A View," "Sail Away" and "Mad About The Boy." His plays were also popular; *Bittersweet* was a major success in London, but the stock market crash in the U. S. forced the play to close prematurely on Broadway. *Private Lives* and *Design For Living* are still peformed in stock and repertoire, and were successful motion pictures. The film version of his play *Cavalcade* won the Academy Award for best picture in 1933.

The war years found Coward devoting himself fully to the war effort, entertaining the troops in Australia and the Far East. His song "London Pride" was a great morale booster (and remains just as popular today in England).

In 1951, Coward appeared in his own nightclub act at the Cafe de Paris, where he was a huge success. Coward's performing breakthrough in the United States began with a television special with Mary Martin in 1955, *Together With Music*. Coward became a frequent attraction in Las Vegas and as a guest on television programs. He was knighted in 1970, and received a special Tony award for his contributions to the theatre. The last project he participated in was the review *Oh, Coward* in 1973, a work that remains popular in Amateur and Stock productions all over the world. He died at his home in Jamaica in 1973.

WALTER DONALDSON

Walter Donaldson was born in New York in 1891. He was a song plugger in his youth, and was fired when he was caught writing his own songs during working hours. His first published song was "Just Try To Picture Me Back Home In Tennessee" in 1915. During World War I, he met Irving Berlin, who became his publisher after the armistice. Donaldson wrote the smash hit "How Ya Gonna Keep 'Em Down On The Farm (Ater They've Seen Paree)" in 1919, and the song sold a million copies of sheet music. Donaldson teamed up with the lyric team of Sam Lewis and Joe Young. Their many hits included "My Mammy," which became Al Jolson's theme.

In 1922, Donaldson began a collaboration with Gus Kahn. Their first song was "My Buddy," a huge success. "Carolina In The Morning," "I Wonder Where My Baby Is Tonight?," "That Certain Party," "My Sweetie Turned Me Down" and "Yes Sir, That's My Baby" followed in quick succession. With Abe Lyman, Donaldson wrote "What Can I Say After I Say I'm Sorry." Donaldson wrote his own lyrics to "At Sundown." Perhaps his biggest selling song was a collaboration with George Whiting, "My Blue Heaven;" five million copies of sheet music was a record for the song's publisher Leo Feist.

In 1928, Donaldson became a publisher himself. The firm of Donaldson, Douglas and Gumble soon issued the score to Eddie Cantor's show *Whoopee*. Such songs as "Love Me Or Leave Me," "Makin' Whoopee" and "My Baby Just Cares For Me" became standards as soon as they left the printing presses.

Donaldson moved to Hollywood to write for the movies in 1930 and remained there until his death in 1947.

VERNON DUKE

Born Vladimir Dukelsky, Duke acquired his anglicized name from George Gershwin. Duke utilized the new name for his popular songs, and used Dukelsky for his concert compositions. While most of his concert music remains obscure, his theatre and popular songs are among the finest in the repertoire.

Duke was born in Russia in 1903. He was educated in Kiev and Odessa, but found his first success as a ballet composer for Serge Diaghilev in France. He first came to the United States in the mid 20s (a partial piano reduction he prepared of "Rhapsody In Blue" dating from this period was recently found in the Warner Bros. Warehouse), and settled here permanently in 1929. His first score for the Broadway stage, *Walk A Little Faster*, was written in 1932, and featured his song "April In Paris." A revue staged in 1934, *Thumbs Up*, yielded the hit "Autumn In New York." Both songs took a while to catch on, but they remain two of the century's biggest hits. He also collaborated with Ira Gershwin on the smash "I Can't Get Started." During 1937, he assisted in the completion of George Gershwin's last film score, *Goldwyn Follies*.

The 40s brought the successful broadway show *Cabin In The Sky*, which showcased the hit song "Taking A Chance On Love." Duke worked on many shows in the coming years that were not successful, but such songs as "The Love I Long For" (Nellie Bly, 1944), "Roundabout" and "Low And Lazy" (Sweet Bye And Bye, 1946) and "Born Too Late" and "Summer Is A-comin' In" (The Littlest Review, 1956) continue to be sung by many cabaret and jazz singers.

Duke died in California in 1969.

SAMMY FAIN

Fain was born Samuel Feinberg in 1902, the son of a cantor. Like Irving Berlin, he was a self-taught pianist, but was writing songs while still in high school. He started out in the stockroom at Shapiro, Bernstein and Co. until the boss heard him sing. Thus began his career as a song demonstrator.

His first hit, "Nobody Knows What A Red-Headed Mama Can Do," was published in 1925. His first steady collaborator was Irving Kahal, and their catalog includes "Let A Smile Be Your Umbrella," "When I Take My Sugar To Tea," "By A Waterfall," "Was That The Human Thing To Do," "I Can Dream, Can't I?" and "I'll Be Seeing You." He was the composer for two beloved Walt Disney animated films, Alice In Wonderland ("I'm Late"), and Peter Pan ("You Can Fly! You Can Fly! You Can Fly!"). His score for *Calamity Jane* produced the classic "Secret Love." He composed theme songs for such films as *Love Is A Many Splendored Thing*, *April Love*, and *A Certain Smile*.

Fain died in Hollywood in 1989.

DOROTHY FIELDS

Dorothy Fields was the daughter of comedian/producer Lew Fields, and both of her brothers, Herbert and Joseph, were librettists. Lew Fields did not want his children to go into show business, and he was particularly upset when Dorothy had theatrical aspirations.

Dorothy, born in New York in 1905, teamed with composer Jimmy McHugh, writing songs for the Cotton Club reviews throughout the twenties. Among the hits for these shows were "Digga Digga Do" and "I Can't Give You Anything But Love." For *Lew Leslie's International Revue*, they wrote "Exactly Like You" and "On the Sunny Side Of The Street." The team moved to Hollywood, and the songs "Don't Blame Me" and "I'm In The Mood For Love" became successes.

Fields later collaborated with Jerome Kern for the scores to four motion pictures. Among the hits that resulted were "I Dream Too Much" "A Fine Romance," "The Way You Look Tonight" and "Remind Me." She returned to Broadway in the late 40's, collaborating with her brother Herbert on the book for *Annie Get Your Gun*. Scores written in the 50s include *A Tree Grows In Brooklyn* ("I'll Buy You A Star") and *By The Beautiful Sea* ("Happy Habit").

Her final collaborator was composer Cy Coleman and the results were the scores for *Seesaw* ("Nobody Does It Like Me") and *Sweet Charity* ("Hey, Big Spender" and "I'm A Brass Band"). Critics noted that the lyricist remained contemporary in outlook and the use of language.

She passed away in 1974.

GEORGE GERSHWIN

Equally at home in the Broadway, motion picture and concert fields, Gershwin's short career was one of the most distinguished in American music. He was born in 1898 and started piano lessons as a boy. While still a teenager, he became a song demonstrator-plugger for the Remick Music Company. He was soon arranging for Irving Berlin and playing rehearsal piano for Jerome Kern. His first Broadway score, *La, La Lucille*, was written in 1919, the same year he wrote one of his biggest hits, "Swanee."

In the 20s, he wrote the scores for several editions of the *George White's Scandals*, and the songs "I'll Build A Stairway To Paradise," "Somebody Loves Me" and "Yankee Doodle Blues" were among his early hits. In 1924, Paul Whiteman commissioned him to compose a concert work to be played in Aeolian Hall; *A Rhapsody In Blue* was the result. This work has become the most popular concert work composed by an American. Gershwin teamed up with his lyricist brother Ira for a number of successful shows, and some of the many hits from this period include "Lady, Be Good," "He Loves And She Loves," "Fascinating Rhythm," "Someone To Watch Over Me," "'S Wonderful," "How Long Has This Been Going On" and "The Man I Love." George also composed a concerto for piano and orchestra, *Concerto in F* and the tone poem *An American In Paris* for the New York Symphony under the baton of Walter Damrosch.

The 30s brought the Gershwin's out to Hollywood for the film musical *Delicious*. In 1934, The Gershwins and DuBose Heyward wrote the folk opera *Porgy And Bess*. Even though it only ran 124 performances on Broadway, the work has since become one of the most beloved American operas, with several new productions in recent years. George and Ira moved to Hollywood permanently in 1936, and such songs as "They Can't Take That Away From Me," "A Foggy Day," "Nice Work If You Can Get It" and "Love Walked In" were composed for a number of now-classic motion pictures.

George died suddenly from an inoperable brain tumor in 1937. His reputation has grown since his death, and several unpublished songs are still waiting to be published and performed.

IRA GERSHWIN

The oldest Gershwin sibling was writing poems and lyrics from boyhood. He was born in 1896. His early lyrics were written under the psuedonym Arthur Francis, the name derived from the first names of his younger brother and his sister. He and George Gershwin became a team in 1924 and remained so until George's death. Ira occasionally wrote songs with other composers, including Vernon Duke ("I Can't Get Started") and Harold Arlen ("Let's Take A Walk Around The Block").

George's death devastated Ira, and it was uncertain whether he would ever work again. However, in 1941, he collaborated with Kurt Weill on the score to *Lady In The Dark*, and such hits as "This Is New," "My Ship" and "The Saga of Jenny" were the result. He further collaborated with Arthur Schwartz ("There's No Holding Me"), Harry Warren ("Shoes With Wings On") and Harold Arlen (the score for the Judy Garland version of *A Star Is Born*). He wrote no new songs after 1960, but adapted lyrics of earlier songs for such artists as Ella Fitzgerald and Frank Sinatra.

He died in California in 1983.

MACK GORDON

Gordon, whose birth name was Morris Gitler, was born in Poland in 1904. He grew up in Brooklyn, and performed in vaudeville as a boy. He began writing songs in his twenties. One of his earliest hits was "Time On My Hands," written with Harold Adamson and Vincent Youmans. From 1931 through 1939, Gordon collaborated with composer Harry Revel. Their many songs included "Did You Ever See A Dream Walking?," "Stay As Sweet As You Are," "Without A Word Of Warning," "You Hit The Spot," "Goodnight, My Love" and "There's a Lull In My Life."

In 1940, Gordon teamed up with Harry Warren for such songs as "You Say The Sweetest Things, Baby," "I Know Why (And So Do You)," "Chattanooga Choo Choo," "There Will Never Be Another You," "My Heart Tells Me," "You'll Never Know" and "The More I See You." Some of his other hits with other writers include "Mam'selle," "Time Alone Will Tell," "You Make Me Feel So Young" and "This Is Always."

He died in New York in 1959.

JOHN GREEN

John Green had a distinguished career as songwriter, arranger, conductor, concert composer, and music administrator. He was born in 1908, and played piano while still a youngster. His parents discouraged him from becoming a full-time musician, and he received a degree in economics from Harvard. His arrangements for the college band so impressed Guy Lombardo that he offered Green a job as arranger. Green wrote his first published song while with Lombardo, "Coquette." After college, he wrote arrangements for Paramount and composed special material for Gertrude Lawrence. One of the songs he wrote for 'G' was "Body And Soul;" "Out Of Nowhere" and "I Cover The Waterfront" followed.

The first of John's unsuccessful Broadway shows was written in 1931, but the show *Here Comes the Bride* included the classic "Hello, My Lover, Goodbye." In addition to his songwriting ("Easy Come, Easy Go," "I Wanna Be Loved," "You're Mine, You," "You And Your Love"), Green led his own orchestra in the 30s. He was a busy conductor on radio and recordings.

By 1940, he'd acquired a reputation as music director for Broadway shows. His success in this vein of the business brought him to Hollywood in 1942, first to MGM, then briefly to Universal for a few movies. In 1948, he was offered the job of running the music department at MGM, a position he held for ten years. By the 60s, he was conducting symphony orchestras in the US and Europe in his own compositions and presentations of film music. He died in California in 1989.

W.C. HANDY

"The Father Of The Blues" was born in Florence, Alabama in 1873. Handy learned several instruments as a child, but his family did not encourage him to become a professional musician, because it was not 'respectable'. Handy followed his own path, joining a minstrel show in 1896. He returned to make his home in the south and became a popular bandleader for dances and concerts. His first published blues was "Memphis Blues." Unfortunately, he was tricked into selling the copyright, and did not realize the vast amount of money generated from that work until the copyright came up for renewal. He continued to compose many blues pieces, among the most popular being "St. Louis Blues," "Beale Street Blues," "Aunt Hagar's Children" and "Chantez Les Bas."

He appeared in vaudeville and special concerts (including a Carnegie Hall concert in 1928 celebrating Negro music), but most of his activity was centered around his publishing company, which is still in business. Later in his life, he concentrated on compiling blues songs for books (the volume, Blues: An Anthology is a classic, and it is still in print) and arranging spirituals. In 1943, he was blinded in an accident, and went into semi-retirement. He died in New York in 1958.

ISHAM JONES

One of the great songwriters in popular music, Jones was also one of the most important dance band leaders in the 20s and 30s. He was born in Coalton, Ohio in 1894. His first published song appeared in 1915. He moved to Chicago, organized a dance band, and was signed to the Brunswick label in 1920. Jones' orchestra was soon recognized as one of the best in the country, and in 1929, the group introduced Hoagy Carmichael's "Star Dust."

Jones' first big songwriting hit was "Swingin' Down The Lane." In 1924, Jones' wife gave him a grand piano for his birthday. Supposedly, he was so concerned about its cost that he sat at the instrument and, within an hour, composed four of the biggest songs of his career; "It Had To Be You," "Spain," "I'll See You In My Dreams" and "The One I Love Belongs To Somebody Else." Among Jones' many other hits were "There Is No Greater Love," "You've Got Me Crying Again," "On The Alamo," "Why Can't This Night Go On Forever" and "I'll Never Have To Dream Again." Jones continued leading the band throughout the early 30s; historians consider the unit he led in 1932-4 to be his greatest band, with arrangements by Gordon Jenkins and Jiggs Noble.

Jones retired in 1936, and the group reformed under the direction of the band's clarinetist/vocalist, Woody Herman. Jones came out of retirement for short periods for personal appearances and/or recordings. He died in Hollywood in 1956.

GUS KAHN

Prolific lyricist Gus Kahn wrote hundreds of songs that eventually became standards. Born in Germany in 1886, he came to the United States when he was five years old, settling in Chicago with his family. His first hit was called "I Wish I Had A Girl," written with composer Grace LeBoy, whom Kahn later married. "Memories" was written with Egbert Van Alstyne, and was a big success. With composer Walter Donaldson, Kahn wrote many hits during the jazz age of the 20s, including "Yes Sir, That's My Baby," "My Baby Just Cares For Me," "Love Me Or Leave Me" and "Makin' Whoopee." With Isham Jones, Kahn wrote "I'll See You In My Dreams," "Swingin' Down The Lane" and "It Had To Be You" (Johnny Mercer's favorite song).

After a collaboration with the Gershwin brothers ("Liza"), Kahn moved to Hollywood and wrote such songs as "Flying Down To Rio," "The Carioca," "Waiting At The Gate For Katy," "San Francisco," "I've Had My Moments" and "You Stepped Out Of A Dream." Kahn's last song was a collaboration with Jerome Kern called "Day Dreaming." He died in 1941.

RAY NOBLE

Noble was already known as an arranger and musical director in his native England when he also added 'songwriter' to his list of accomplishments. Born in 1908, Noble won an arranging contest in his early 20s, which helped establish his bandleading career. He made hundreds of highly prized dance recordings for HMV, and broadcast regularly over the BBC.

In 1934, he decided to bring his orchestra to the United States, but union regulations prohibited him from doing so. Noble hired Glenn Miller to arrange and contract the band with Amercian players, and the resulting ensemble was popular from the start. Part of the band's repertoire was the wonderful songs that Noble wrote during the 30s which included "The Very Thought Of You," "The Touch Of Your Lips," "Love Locked Out" and "Love Is The Sweetest Thing."

Noble eventually moved to the West Coast, and while continuing to lead an orchestra, he became a radio personality on the Burns and Allen and Edgar Bergen radio shows. Eventually he gave up his activities to retire to an island in the Mediterranean. He died in California in 1978.

MITCHELL PARISH

Born in Shreveport, Louisiana in 1900, Parish was a lyricist best known for putting lyrics to melodies that had already become popular as instrumental compositions. Among the many songs he lyricised were "Star Dust," "Mood Indigo," "Sophisticated Lady," "Stairway To The Stars," "Organ Grinder's Swing," "Don't Be That Way," "Deep Purple," "Moonlight Serenade," "The Syncopated Clock," "Serenata," "Sleigh Ride," "Tzena, Tzena, Tzena" and "Ciao, Ciao, Bambino." In 1987, Parish was honored with his own review on Broadway called *Star Dust*, and a commemorative large sized book of his lyrics. He died in New York in 1993.

ANDY RAZAF

One of the great lyricists of American popular song was related to the Queen of Madagascar. Andrea Paul Razafinkeriefo was born in Washington, D.C. in 1895. Razaf shortened his name when he began contributing poetry to newspapers as a teenager. He worked at a variety of jobs while writing lyrics, including an elevator operator and a baseball player.

His first song to appear in a Broadway show was "Baltimo'" for *The Passing Show of 1913*; Razaf was seventeen years old. In the 20s, he found a collaborator in Thomas 'Fats' Waller. Among the many songs they wrote together were "Ain't Misbehavin," "Honeysuckle Rose," "Black And Blue," "Blue Turning Gray Over You," "Keepin' Out Of Mischief Now," "Willow Tree" and "I've Got A Feeling I'm Falling." Razaf also wrote many songs with Eubie Blake ("Memories Of You," "You're Lucky To Me"). Other collaborators included J.C. Johnson ("Louisiana") and Paul Denniker ("S'posin'").

During the big band era, he contributed lyrics to "Stompin' At The Savoy" and "In the Mood." During the 40s, Razaf found work increasingly difficult to obtain. He ran for City Council in Englewood, N.J., losing in a bitterly contested election. From 1951, he was in poor health until his death in 1973. He was elected into The Songwriter's Hall of Fame in 1972.

HARRY REVEL

Born in London, England in 1905, Revel studied at the prestigious Guildhall School Of Music. He went to Europe at 15 and played in dance orchestras. While there, he also established himself as a composer of light orchestral music.

In 1929, he relocated to New York, where he met vaudevillian Mack Gordon. Their ten-year songwriting collaboration started on Broadway and eventually, the team signed a contract to write songs for Paramount Pictures. Besides the song titles already cited in Gordon's biography, the team wrote "May I," "Love Thy Neighbor," "With My Eyes Wide Open, I'm Dreaming" and "Meet The Beat Of My Heart."

Revel was an officer in the Air Force during World War II, assigned to put together entertainment units to bolster morale for the troops. He found a new collaborator in Mort Greene, writing several songs including "Remember Me To Carolina." He also collaborated with Arnold Horwitt for the score to the Broadway show *Are You With It*. Revel's last hit was originally a composition for theramin; outfitted with lyrics by Bennie Benjamin and George David Weiss, the song "Jet" was popularized by Nat King Cole in 1951.

Revel died in New York in 1958.

HARRY VON TILZER

A pioneer publisher and songwriter, Von Tilzer wrote prolifically and in many different genres. Many of his songs became hits due to his talent for song plugging. One of his best pluggers became a hitmaking songwriter himself - Irving Berlin.

Born Harry Gumm in Detroit, Michigan in 1872, Von Tilzer was performing on stages and circuses by the time he was fourteen. Vaudevillian Lottie Gilson encouraged him to move to New York and concentrate on his songwriting. The next few years were hard, but the young man learned his craft. In 1900, he wrote "A Bird In A Gilded Cage," a song that sold two million copies of sheet music.

In 1902, he started his own publishing company, and turned out hit after hit. "Wait Till The Sun Shines, Nellie," "I Want A Girl Just Like The Girl That Married Dear Old Dad" and "All Alone" are songs that are still performed today. Overall, Von Tilzer wrote over one hundred songs that sold over 500,000 copies each. His office remained open, still publishing songs, until his death in 1946.

FATS WALLER

One of the great pianists and entertainers of the century, Waller is also one of its greatest songwriters. Born Thomas Waller in New York in 1904, Waller's father was a lay preacher in Harlem. Fats studied both piano and organ, and became accompanist at various silent movie theatres. He was fortunate to meet and receive encouragement from master pianists Willie 'The Lion' Smith and James P. Johnson. Johnson became the boy's mentor, and Fats was soon known all over New York music circles.

Fats made his first recordings in 1922, and by 1923 was a published composer. By the late 20s, the major jazz figures were recording such Waller compositions as "Stealin' Apples" and "Crazy 'Bout My Baby." With lyricist Andy Razaf, he wrote "Honeysuckle Rose," "Black And Blue" and "Ain't Misbehavin'." Increasingly, Waller became a radio and recording star, with a long-term recording contract with RCA and several radio shows of his own. In 1938, he toured Europe for the first time, where he was received like royalty. On his return trip in 1939 he composed "The London Suite."

His last years saw him in Hollywood in the motion picture *Stormy Weather*, in his own concert at Carnegie Hall, and represented on Broadway with the score to *Early To Bed*. He died in Kansas City in 1943.

HARRY WARREN

Perhaps one of the greatest melodists in the song field, Warren is still relatively unknown today. His songs, however, remain some of the most performed and beloved of this century. He was born Salvatore Guaragna in Brooklyn in 1893. He became a stage hand at the Liberty Theatre in Brooklyn, and later worked as an all-around utility man at the Vitagraph Studios.

His first published song was "Rose Of The Rio Grande" in 1922. It became a big hit, and Warren was on his way. During the 20s, he wrote "I Love My Baby (My Baby Loves Me)," "Clementine" and "Nagasaki." For the Broadway show *Sweet And Low*, he wrote "Would You Like To Take A Walk" and "Cheerful Little Earful." "You're My Everything" and "I Found A Million Dollar Baby (In A Five And Ten Cent Store)" followed.

Like most Broadway songwriters, he moved to Hollywood in 1932 when Warner Bros. studios offered him a contract. He was teamed with lyricist Al Dubin, and the new team wrote some of the biggest hits of the decade. These include "Shuffle Off To Buffalo," "Forty-Second Street," "You're Getting To Be A Habit With Me," "The Gold Diggers' Song (We're In The Money)," "I Only Have Eyes For You," "Lullaby Of Broadway" and "September In The Rain." When Dubin returned to New York, Warren paired up with Johnny Mercer, and the songs they wrote included "You Must Have Been A Beautiful Baby" and "Jeepers Creepers."

In 1940, Warren moved to the Twentieth Century Fox studios and teamed up with Mack Gordon. The classic songs continued with "Chatanooga Choo Choo," "At Last," "I Know Why (And So Do You)," "Serenade In Blue," "There'll Never Be Another You," "I Had The Craziest Dream," "The More I See You" and "You'll Never Know." Moving to MGM, Warren wrote "This Heart Of Mine," "Wait And See" and "On The Atchison, Topeka and The Santa Fe."

In the 50s, he wrote a number of beautiful songs for various projects. "That's Amore" and "An Affair To Remember" were the most popular of these later songs. Warren won three Academy Awards for his work.

He died in Los Angeles in 1982, while a stage version of *42nd Street* was doing turnaway business on Broadway.

KURT WEILL

The son of a cantor, Weill was born in Germany in 1900. He received a thorough grounding in piano, theory and composition, and was part of an exclusive master class in composition taught by Ferrucio Busoni in 1921. His compositions during this period include a violin concerto and a symphony. Weill was regarded as an important new composer when he met playwright Bertolt Brecht in 1927 and began one of the great collaborations in German opera. Among their works are *The Threepenny Opera* and *The Rise And Fall Of The City Of Mahagonny*, both great successes until further productions were banned by the Nazis.

Weill left Germany and after living in Switzerland and London for short periods, moved to the United States. With him was his wife, actress Lotte Lenya (who was also one of the finest interpreters of his music).

In America, Weill wrote for radio, Hollywood and the concert hall, but his true love was the theatre. He was newly challenged by the demands of the Broadway stage and its audience. His first American stage work, *Johnny Johnson*, was an anti-war play with music that was critically acclaimed. *Knickerbocker Holiday* premiered in 1938, and "September Song" became Weill's first American song hit. *Lady In the Dark* was also a big success, with such songs as "This Is New," "The Saga Of Jenny" and "My Ship." "Speak Low" was the big hit from the show *One Touch Of Venus*.

Weill wanted to write an opera for Broadway, and the result, *Street Scene*, was a high water-mark for Weill. This work has become increasingly popular in opera houses all over the world. *Lost In The Stars*, based on the novel *Cry The Beloved Country*, was another personal and professional success.

Weill was working on a stage version of *Huckleberry Finn* when he succumbed to a heart attack and died in New York in 1950. The Kurt Weill Foundation, located in New York, has begun to issue authoratative volumes of his music. Weill's popularity continues to grow.

RICHARD WHITING

Whiting was born in Peoria, Illinois in 1891. While in high school, he wrote his first songs. He became the professional manager of the Detroit office of the Jerome Remick Publishing Company. Among the many hits that Whiting and his lyricist Raymond Egan wrote were the blockbusters "Till We Meet Again," "The Japanese Sandman" and "Ain't We Got Fun." With other collaborators, Whiting wrote "Sleepy Time Gal," "Breezin' Along With The Breeze" and "She's Funny That Way."

Whiting was one of many songwriters to relocate to Hollywood to write for motion pictures. He wrote such durable songs as "Guilty," "Louise," "True Blue Lou," "Beyond The Blue Horizon," "My Ideal" and "One Hour With You." Whiting wrote the score for his only Broadway show, *Take A Chance*, which featured "You're An Old Smoothie."

Back in Hollywood, Whiting wrote "On The Good Ship Lollypop" for Shirley Temple, "Too Marvelous For Words" and "Hooray For Hollywood." He died in Beverly Hills in 1937. Both of his daughters went into show business, and Margaret Whiting continues to favor her father's songs when she performs.

VINCENT YOUMANS

Youmans wrote some of the most enduring popular songs of the century, but retired at an early age to write concert music. He was born in New York in 1898. During World War I, he enlisted in the Navy, and became rehearsal pianist for Navy morale shows. After the war, he became a song plugger for Remick. He received invaluable training when he worked with Victor Herbert on the show *Oui Madam* in 1920. Unfortunately, the show never opened on Broadway.

One of his earliest collaborators was Ira Gershwin, and in 1921, they wrote the score to *Two Little Girls* In Blue. It was the first Broadway show for both of them, and one of the songs became a big hit, "Oh, Me! Oh, My! (Oh, You!)." By 1924, Youmans hit his stride. In 1925, with Irving Caesar, Youmans wrote the score for one of the biggest hit shows of the decade, *No, No, Nanette*, which featured "Tea For Two" and "I Want To Be Happy." "I Know That You Know" was written for the show *Oh, Please. Hit The Deck*, a show Youmans also produced, had such standards as "Hallelujah" and "Sometimes I'm Happy."

Unfortunately, Youmans' remaining Broadway shows were unsuccessful, and yet the scores are some of the richest in the American theatre of the 20's. *Great Day* was a 36 performance flop, which included the title song, "More Than You Know" and "Without A Song." The Florenz Ziegfeld show *Smiles* included "Time On My Hands." Youmans produced *Through The Years*, the title song of which was the personal favorite of his many compositions. The show ran 20 performances.

Youmans went to Hollywood in 1933 to write the score for the film *Flying Down To Rio*. Now remembered as the first film to feature Fred Astaire and Ginger Rogers, the score included "The Carioca." Afterward, Youmans went to Colorado to recover from tuberculosis. He studied composition and aspired to write orchestral music and operettas. He never wrote another score for Broadway or Hollywood, and his orchestral music has never been found. He died in Colorado in 1946.

200 OF THE BEST SONGS FROM
RAGTIME
ARTIST INDEX
& EARLY JAZZ

CANNONBALL ADDERLEY I'VE TOLD EV'RY LITTLE STAR

GENE AMMONS OL' MAN RIVER

WHY WAS I BORN?

IVIE ANDERSON ON THE SUNNY SIDE OF THE STREET

LOUIS ARMSTRONG BASIN STREET BLUES

DO YOU KNOW WHAT IT MEANS
TO MISS NEW ORLEANS

SHINE

ST. LOUIS BLUES

FRED ASTAIRE I'M PUTTING ALL MY EGGS IN ONE BASKET

PUTTIN' ON THE RITZ

GENE AUSTIN FIVE FOOT TWO, EYES OF BLUE

MILDRED BAILEY SQUEEZE ME

CHET BAKER LOOK FOR THE SILVER LINING

THE TOUCH OF YOUR LIPS

WITH A SONG IN MY HEART

COUNT BASIE AS LONG AS I LIVE

I'M CONFESSIN'

BIX BEIDERBECKE COPENHAGEN

GEORGE BENSON WALKIN' MY BABY BACK HOME

THE BOSWELL SISTERS I CAN'T GIVE YOU ANYTHING BUT LOVE

CLIFFORD BROWN CAN'T HELP LOVIN' DAT MAN

I CAN DREAM, CAN'T I?

SMOKE GETS IN YOUR EYES

THE WAY YOU LOOK TONIGHT

CHICK BULLOCK ANNIE DOESN'T LIVE HERE ANYMORE

HOAGY CARMICHAEL ROCKIN' CHAIR

BENNY CARTER WHEN LIGHTS ARE LOW

THE CASA LOMA ORCHESTRA SMOKE RINGS

UNDER A BLANKET OF BLUE

JUNE CHRISTY LOVE IS JUST AROUND THE CORNER

ROSEMARY CLOONEY HOW ABOUT ME?

NAT KING COLE BLAME IT ON MY YOUTH

INDIANA

THE LONESOME ROAD

MAKIN' WHOOPEE!

WHEN I TAKE MY SUGAR TO TEA

YOU'RE MY EVERYTHING

CY COLEMAN LULLABY OF THE LEAVES

JOHN COLTRANE I'LL GET BY

I'M A DREAMER AREN'T WE ALL

IT'S EASY TO REMEMBER

MY IDEAL

YOU ARE TOO BEAUTIFUL

CHRIS CONNOR WHAT IS THERE TO SAY

BING CROSBY DOWN BY THE RIVER

MOONLIGHT BAY

PLEASE

THANKS

WHERE THE BLUE OF THE NIGHT

MILES DAVIS BYE BYE BLACKBIRD

LOVE ME OR LEAVE ME

DOROTHY DELL DO I LOVE YOU

BUDDY DE FRANCO DANCING ON THE CEILING

OUT OF NOWHERE

LOU DONALDSON THE BEST THINGS IN LIFE ARE FREE

KENNY DORHAM	WHY DO I LOVE YOU?	**BENNY GOODMAN**	ALWAYS
BILLY ECKSTINE	YOU CALL IT MADNESS		AVALON
DUKE ELLINGTON	BLACK AND TAN FANTASY		DINAH
	DROP ME OFF IN HARLEM		EVERYBODY LOVES MY BABY
	IT DON'T MEAN A THING		THE GLORY OF LOVE
	MOOD INDIGO		I NEVER KNEW
	RING DEM BELLS		I'VE GOT A FEELING I'M FALLING
	SOLITUDE		LET'S DANCE
	SOPHISTICATED LADY		MOONGLOW
BILL EVANS	DANNY BOY		ROSE OF WASHINGTON SQUARE
	MY MELANCHOLY BABY		ROSE ROOM
TAL FARLOW	ISN'T IT ROMANTIC?		ROYAL GARDEN BLUES
ROBERT FARNON	YOU'RE THE CREAM IN MY COFFEE		SOMETIMES I'M HAPPY
ELLA FITZGERALD	DON'T BE THAT WAY		YOU BROUGHT A NEW KIND OF LOVE TO ME
	DREAM A LITTLE DREAM OF ME	**EDMOND HALL**	IN A SHANTY IN OLD SHANTY TOWN
	HERE IN MY ARMS	**JIM HALL**	SOFTLY AS IN A MORNING SUNRISE
	LITTLE WHITE LIES	**COLEMAN HAWKINS**	THE BLUE ROOM
	SOMEBODY LOVES ME		BODY AND SOUL
	YOU HIT THE SPOT		BUGLE CALL RAG
JUDY GARLAND	OH! YOU BEAUTIFUL DOLL		I WISHED ON THE MOON
STAN GETZ	BYE BYE BLUES		MY BLUE HEAVEN
	THOU SWELL		SHEIK OF ARABY
DIZZY GILLESPIE	GET HAPPY		THE WORLD IS WAITING FOR THE SUNRISE
	LOVER, COME BACK TO ME	**EARL HINES**	ROSETTA
	WRAP YOUR TROUBLES IN DREAMS	**BILLIE HOLIDAY**	ALL OF ME
BENNY GOLSON	YOU'RE MINE, YOU!		I CRIED FOR YOU
PAUL GONSALVES	YESTERDAYS		I'M YOURS
			MISS BROWN TO YOU
			SAY IT ISN'T SO
		FREDDIE HUBBARD	WITHOUT A SONG

236

MAHALIA JACKSON	AMAZING GRACE	**BILL PERKINS**	SONG OF THE ISLANDS
	BATTLE HYMN OF THE REPUBLIC	**OSCAR PETERSON**	THE BIRTH OF THE BLUES
	NOBODY KNOWS THE TROUBLE I'VE SEEN		I'VE GOT THE WORLD ON A STRING
DICK JACOBS	FASCINATION		LET'S FALL IN LOVE
HARRY JAMES	I'M ALWAYS CHASING RAINBOWS		POOR BUTTERFLY
	YOU MADE ME LOVE YOU	**BUD POWELL**	MY OLD FLAME
JACK JENNEY	STAR DUST	**DON REDMAN**	GEE BABY, AIN'T I GOOD TO YOU
AL JOLSON	I'M SITTING ON TOP OF THE WORLD	**ADRIAN ROLLINI**	SUGAR
STAN KENTON	THE THRILL IS GONE	**SONNY ROLLINS**	MORE THAN YOU KNOW
TEDDI KING	A SHIP WITHOUT A SAIL		SOMEDAY I'LL FIND YOU
GENE KRUPA	THERE'LL BE SOME CHANGES MADE		STAY AS SWEET AS YOU ARE
FRANKIE LAINE	NEVERTHELESS	**GEORGE SHEARING**	THEY DIDN'T BELIEVE ME
TED LEWIS	WHEN MY BABY SMILES AT ME		WHAT'LL I DO
JIMMIE LUNCEFORD	MARGIE	**ZOOT SIMS**	SEPTEMBER SONG
MARIAN McPARTLAND	JUST ONE MORE CHANCE	**FRANK SINATRA**	BLUE SKIES
CARMEN McRAE	MAD ABOUT THE BOY		I DON'T STAND A GHOST OF A CHANCE
GLENN MILLER	HALLELUJAH		I WON'T DANCE
THELONIOUS MONK	JUST A GIGOLO		IT ALL DEPENDS ON YOU
WES MONTGOMERY	FALLING IN LOVE WITH LOVE		MEAN TO ME
LEE MORGAN	ILL WIND		MOONLIGHT ON THE GANGES
BENNIE MOTEN	MOTEN SWING		THE NIGHT IS YOUNG
NEW ORLEANS RHYTHM KINGS	MILENBERG JOYS		ROSES OF PICARDY
RED NORVO	REMEMBER		SHE'S FUNNY THAT WAY
ANITA O'DAY	HAVE YOU MET MISS JONES?	**KATE SMITH**	MOON SONG
	IN A LITTLE SPANISH TOWN	**MAMIE SMITH**	ROYAL GARDEN BLUES
CHARLIE PARKER	AFTER YOU'VE GONE	**MAXINE SULLIVAN**	LOCH LOMOND
	AUTUMN IN NEW YORK	**WILBUR SWEATMAN**	JA-DA
	EAST OF THE SUN		
	HOW DEEP IS THE OCEAN		
	I CAN'T BELIEVE THAT YOU'RE IN LOVE WITH ME		
	LOVER		
	THE SONG IS YOU		

ART TATUM	AUNT HAGAR'S BLUES
	COCKTAILS FOR TWO
	DARDANELLA
	LITTLE MAN YOU'VE HAD A BUSY DAY
	MY HEART STOOD STILL
	TIGER RAG
	YOU TOOK ADVANTAGE OF ME
BILLY TAYLOR	JUST IMAGINE
CLARK TERRY	AMONG MY SOUVENIRS
FRANK TRUMBAUER	SINGIN' THE BLUES TILL MY DADDY COMES HOME
SOPHIE TUCKER	SOME OF THESE DAYS
SARAH VAUGHAN	DON'T WORRY 'BOUT ME
	EVERYTHING I HAVE IS YOURS
	LITTLE GIRL BLUE
	MY KINDA LOVE
	PENTHOUSE SERENADE
FATS WALLER	AIN'T MISBEHAVIN'
	HONEYSUCKLE ROSE
	THE JOINT IS JUMPIN'
	MEMORIES OF YOU
DINAH WASHINGTON	FOR ALL WE KNOW
PAUL WHITEMAN	SAN
	WHISPERING
ERNIE WILKINS	YOU'RE DRIVING ME CRAZY!
TEDDY WILSON	EXACTLY LIKE YOU
	SWEET SUE - JUST YOU
	WHEN YOU AND I WERE YOUNG, MAGGIE
PHIL WOODS	LAST NIGHT WHEN WE WERE YOUNG
LESTER YOUNG	IT'S THE TALK OF THE TOWN
	PRISONER OF LOVE

THE ULTIMATE COLLECTION OF
FAKE BOOKS

The Ultimate Fake Book – 3rd Edition

Includes over 1,200 hits: Blue Skies • Body and Soul • Theme from Cheers • Endless Love • A Foggy Day • Isn't It Romantic? • Memory • Mona Lisa • Moon River • Operator • Piano Man • Roxanne • Satin Doll • Shout • Small World • Speak Softly, Love • Strawberry Fields Forever • Tears in Heaven • Unforgettable • hundreds more!

00240024 C Edition $45.00
00240026 Bb Edition $45.00
00240025 Eb Edition $45.00

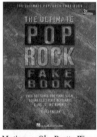

Best Fake Book Ever – 2nd Edition

More than 1000 songs from all styles of music, including: All My Loving • American Pie • At the Hop • Cabaret • Dust in the Wind • Fever • Free Bird • From a Distance • Hello, Dolly! • Hey Jude • King of the Road • Longer • Misty • Route 66 • Sentimental Journey • Somebody • Song Sung Blue • Spinning Wheel • Unchained Melody • We Will Rock You • What a Wonderful World • Wooly Bully • Y.M.C.A. • You're So Vain • and hundreds more.

00290239 C Edition $45.00
00240083 Bb Edition $45.00
00240084 Eb Edition $45.00

The Ultimate Pop/Rock Fake Book – 3rd Edition

Over 500 pop standards and contemporary hits, including: Addicted to Love • All Shook Up • Another One Bites the Dust • Crocodile Rock • Crying • Don't Know Much • Dust in the Wind • Earth Angel • Every Breath You Take • Hero • Hey Jude • Hold My Hand • Imagine • Layla • The Loco-Motion • Oh, Pretty Woman • On Broadway • Spinning Wheel • Stand by Me • Stayin' Alive • Tears in Heaven • True Colors • The Twist • Vision of Love • A Whole New World • Wild Thing • Wooly Bully • Yesterday • and many more!

00240099 $39.95

Latin Fake Book

Over 500 Latin songs in many styles, including mambos, sambas, cha cha chás, rhumbas, tangos, salsa, Latin pop and rock, and more. Songs include: Adiós • Água De Beber • Amapola • Antigua • Babalú • Bésame Mucho • Brazil • Cachita • Desafinado • Dindi • El Triste • Ella • Flamingo • Frenesí • The Girl from Ipanema • La Cucaracha • La Fiesta • Livin' La Vida Loca • Malagueña • Mambo No. 5 • Mambo No. 8 • Manteca • Maria Elena • One Note Samba • Poinciana • Similau • Spanish Eyes • Speak Low • St. Thomas • Tico Tico • Triste • Wave • more!

00240146 $35.00

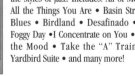

The Ultimate Jazz Fake Book

Over 625 jazz classics spanning more than nine decades and representing all the styles of jazz. Includes: All of Me • All the Things You Are • Basin Street Blues • Birdland • Desafinado • A Foggy Day •I Concentrate on You • In the Mood • Take the "A" Train • Yardbird Suite • and many more!

00240079 C Edition $39.95
00240080 Bb Edition $39.95
00240081 Eb Edition $39.95

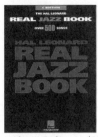

The Hal Leonard Real Jazz Book

A unique collection of jazz material in a wide variety of styles with no song duplication from The Ultimate Jazz Fake Book! Includes over 500 songs including a great deal of hard-to-find repertoire and a significant number of songs which have never before been printed.

00240097 C Edition $39.95
00240122 Bb Edition $39.95
00240123 Eb Edition $39.95

The Ultimate Broadway Fake Book – 4th Edition

More than 670 show-stoppers from over 200 shows! Includes: Ain't Misbehavin' • All I Ask of You • As If We Never Said Goodbye • Bewitched • Camelot • Memory • Don't Cry for Me Argentina • Edelweiss • I Dreamed a Dream • If I Were a Rich Man • Oklahoma • People • Seasons of Love • Send in the Clowns • Someone • What I Did for Love • and more.

00240046 $39.95

The Classical Fake Book

An unprecedented, amazingly comprehensive reference of over 650 classical themes and melodies for all classical music lovers. Includes everything from Renaissance music to Vivaldi and Mozart to Mendelssohn. Lyrics in the original language are included when appropriate.

00240044 $24.95

R&B Fake Book

This terrific fake book features more than 250 classic R&B hits: Baby Love • Best of My Love • Dancing in the Street • Easy • Get Ready • Heatwave • Here and Now • Just Once • Let's Get It On • The Loco-Motion • (You Make Me Feel Like) A Natural Woman • One Sweet Day • Papa Was a Rollin' Stone • Save the Best for Last • September • Sexual Healing • Shop Around • Smoke Gets in Your Eyes • Still • Tell It Like It Is • Up on the Roof • Walk on By • What's Going On • more!

00240107 C Edition $25.00

The Ultimate Country Fake Book – 4th Edition

This 4th edition includes even more of your favorite country hits – over 700 songs by country superstars of yesterday and today: Achy Breaky Heart (Don't Tell My Heart) • Always on My Mind • Are You Lonesome Tonight? • Boot Scootin' Boogie • Crazy • Daddy Sang Bass • Down at the Twist and Shout • Elvira • Forever and Ever, Amen • Friends in Low Places • The Gambler • Jambalaya • King of the Road • Rocky Top • Sixteen Tons • There's a Tear in My Beer • What's Forever For • Your Cheatin' Heart • and more.

00240049 $39.95

Wedding & Love Fake Book

Over 400 classic and contemporary songs, including: All for Love • All I Ask of You • Anniversary Song • Ave Maria • Can You Feel the Love Tonight • Endless Love • Forever and Ever, Amen • Forever in Love • I Wanna Be Loved • It Could Happen to You • Misty • My Heart Will Go On • So in Love • Through the Years • Vision of Love • and more.

00240041 $29.95

The Irving Berlin Fake Book

Over 150 Berlin songs, including: Alexander's Ragtime Band • Always • Blue Skies • Easter Parade • God Bless America • Happy Holiday • Heat Wave • I've Got My Love to Keep Me Warm • Puttin' on the Ritz • White Christmas • and more.

00240043 $19.95

Classic Rock Fake Book

This new fake book is a great compilation of more than 250 terrific songs of the rock era, arranged for piano, voice, guitar and all C instruments. Includes: All Right Now • American Woman • Birthday • Born to Be Wild • Brown Eyed Girl • Free Bird • Honesty • I Shot the Sheriff • I Want You to Want Me • Imagine • It's Still Rock and Roll to Me • Lay Down Sally • Layla • Magic Carpet Ride • My Generation • Rikki Don't Lose That Number • Rock and Roll All Nite • Spinning Wheel • Sweet Home Alabama • White Room • We Will Rock You • lots more!

00240108 $24.95

Gospel's Greatest Fake Book

An excellent resource for Gospel titles with over 450 songs, including: Amazing Grace • At the Cross • Behold the Lamb • Blessed Assurance • He Touched Me • Heavenly Sunlight • His Eye Is on the Sparrow • Holy Ground • How Great Thou Art • I Saw the Light • I'd Rather Have Jesus • In the Garden • Joshua (Fit the Battle of Jericho) • Just a Closer Walk with Thee • Lord, I'm Coming Home • Midnight Cry • Morning Has Broken • My Tribute • Near the Cross • The Old Rugged Cross • Precious Memories • Rock of Ages • Shall We Gather at the River? • What a Friend We Have in Jesus • and more.

00240136 $24.95

FOR MORE INFORMATION, SEE YOUR LOCAL MUSIC DEALER,
OR WRITE TO:

HAL•LEONARD®
CORPORATION
7777 W. BLUEMOUND RD. P.O. BOX 13819 MILWAUKEE, WI 53213

http://www.halleonard.com

Prices, contents and availabilty subject to change without notice

0700

JAZZ IMPROVISATION WORKSHOP

An exciting new improvisation method designed for all levels of players – from the absolute beginner to the experienced performer. Instructional volumes can be used individually or in a group/classroom environment. Play-along song collections feature musical variety, top-notch rhythm section accompaniment, great tunes, and performance of each head as well as choruses for improvisation. Each book includes a play-along CD.

PATTERNS FOR BEGINNING IMPROVISATION

For All Instruments • by Frank Mantooth

FROM THE BEGINNING
This beginning improvisation method is designed for students who are beginners in jazz – no prior jazz experience is necessary to use this book. The patterns begin simply and gradually increase in difficulty.
00841100 C Inst
00841101 Bb Inst
00841102 Eb Inst
00841103 Bass Clef

MOVIN' ON TO THE BLUES
This method for blues improvisation is designed for students with minimal jazz experience. Simple patterns are presented with easy, but frequently encountered progressions.
00841104 C Inst
00841105 Bb Inst
00841106 Eb Inst
00841107 Bass Clef

JAZZ STANDARDS PLAY-ALONG COLLECTIONS

JAZZ CLASSIC STANDARDS
15 songs, including: All Of Me • Don't Get Around Much Anymore • Milestones • My Funny Valentine • Opus One • When I Fall In Love • and more.
00841120 C Inst
00841121 Bb Inst
00841122 Eb Inst
00841123 Bass Clef

JAZZ FAVORITES
15 songs, including: Bewitched • Bye Bye Blackbird • How High The Moon • Now's The Time • Speak Low • and more.
00841124 C Inst
00841125 Bb Inst
00841126 Eb Inst
00841127 Bass Clef

ESSENTIAL JAZZ STANDARDS
15 songs, including: The Girl From Ipanema • Groovin' High • Have You Met Miss Jones? • It Could Happen To You • It Might As Well Be Spring • Long Ago And Far Away • A Night In Tunisia • Stella By Starlight • and more.
00841128 C Inst
00841129 Bb Inst
00841130 Eb Inst
00841131 Bass Clef

JAZZ GEMS
15 songs, including: All The Things You Are • Bluesette • Epistrophy • How Insensitive • My Funny Valentine • My Romance • Satin Doll • Summer Samba (So Nice) • Tangerine • and more.
00841132 C Inst
00841133 Bb Inst
00841134 Eb Inst
00841135 Bass Clef

FOR MORE INFORMATION, SEE YOUR LOCAL MUSIC DEALER, OR WRITE TO:

HAL•LEONARD®
CORPORATION
7777 W. BLUEMOUND RD. P.O. BOX 13819 MILWAUKEE, WI 53213

Visit Hal Leonard on the internet at http://www.halleonard.com

Prices, contents, and availability subject to change without notice. Some products may not be available outside the U.S.A.   0300

ARTIST TRANSCRIPTIONS®

Artist Transcriptions are authentic, note-for-note transcriptions of the hottest artists in jazz, pop, and rock today. These outstanding, accurate arrangements are in an easy-to-read format which includes all essential lines. Artist Transcriptions can be used to perform, sequence or reference.

GUITAR & BASS

The Guitar Book of Pierre Bensusan
00699072.................................$19.95

Ron Carter – Acoustic Bass
00672331.................................$16.95

**Charley Christian –
The Art of Jazz Guitar**
00026704 .... $8.95

Stanley Clarke Collection
00672307.................................$19.95

Al Di Meola – Cielo E Terra
00604041.................................$14.95

**Al Di Meola –
Friday Night in San Francisco**
00660115.................................$14.95

Al Di Meola – Music, Words, Pictures
00604043.................................$14.95

Kevin Eubanks Guitar Collection
00672319.................................$19.95

The Jazz Style of Tal Farlow
00673245.................................$19.95

Bela Fleck and the Flecktones
00672359 Melody/Lyrics/Chords....$14.95

David Friesen – Departure
00673221.................................$14.95

David Friesen – Years Through Time
00673253.................................$14.95

Best Of Frank Gambale
00672336.................................$22.95

Jim Hall – Jazz Guitar Environments
00699389 Book/CD $19.95

Jim Hall – Exploring Jazz Guitar
00699306.................................$16.95

Scott Henderson Guitar Book
00699330.................................$19.95

**Allan Holdsworth –
Reaching for the Uncommon Chord**
00604049.................................$14.95

Leo Kottke – Eight Songs
00699215.................................$14.95

Wes Montgomery – Guitar Transcriptions
00675536.................................$14.95

Joe Pass Collection
00672353.................................$16.95

John Patitucci
00673216.................................$14.95

Django Reinhardt Anthology
00027083.................................$14.95

The Genius of Django Reinhardt
00026711.................................$10.95

Django Reinhardt – A Treasury of Songs
00026715.................................$12.95

**John Renbourn – The Nine Maidens,
The Hermit, Stefan and John**
00699071.................................$12.95

Great Rockabilly Guitar Solos
00692820.................................$14.95

John Scofield – Guitar Transcriptions
00603390.................................$16.95

**Andres Segovia –
20 Studies for the Guitar**
00006362 Book/Cassette $14.95

Johnny Smith Guitar Solos
00672374.................................$14.95

Mike Stern Guitar Book
00673224.................................$16.95

Mark Whitfield
00672320.................................$19.95

Jack Wilkins – Windows
00673249.................................$14.95

Gary Willis Collection
00672337.................................$19.95

CLARINET

Buddy De Franco Collection
00672423.................................$19.95

FLUTE

James Newton – Improvising Flute
00660108.................................$14.95

The Lew Tabackin Collection
00672455.................................$19.95

TROMBONE

J.J. Johnson Collection
00672332.................................$19.95

TRUMPET

Randy Brecker
00673234.................................$14.95

**The Brecker Brothers...
And All Their Jazz**
00672351.................................$19.95

Best of the Brecker Brothers
00672447.................................$19.95

Miles Davis – Standards
00672450.................................$19.95

Freddie Hubbard
00673214.................................$14.95

Tom Harrell Jazz Trumpet
00672382.................................$19.95

Jazz Trumpet Solos
00672363................................. $9.95

PIANO & KEYBOARD

Monty Alexander Collection
00672338.................................$19.95

Kenny Barron Collection
00672318.................................$22.95

Warren Bernhardt Collection
00672364.................................$19.95

Cyrus Chesnut Collection
00672437.................................$19.95

Billy Childs Collection
00672342.................................$19.95

Chick Corea – Elektric Band
00603126.................................$15.95

Chick Corea – Paint the World
00672300.................................$12.95

Bill Evans Collection
00672365.................................$19.95

Benny Green Collection
00672329.................................$19.95

Herbie Hancock Collection
00672419.................................$19.95

Gene Harris Collection
00672446.................................$19.95

Ahmad Jamal Collection
00672322.................................$22.95

Jazz Master Classics for Piano
00672354.................................$14.95

**Thelonious Monk – Intermediate
Piano Solos**
00672392.................................$12.95

Jelly Roll Morton – The Piano Rolls
00672433.................................$12.95

Michel Petrucciani
00673226.................................$17.95

Bud Powell Classics
00672371.................................$19.95

André Previn Collection
00672437.................................$19.95

Horace Silver Collection
00672303.................................$19.95

Art Tatum Collection
00672316.................................$22.95

Art Tatum Solo Book
00672355.................................$19.95

Billy Taylor Collection
00672357.................................$24.95

McCoy Tyner
00673215.................................$14.95

Cedar Walton Collection
00672321.................................$19.95

SAXOPHONE

Julian "Cannonball" Adderly Collection
00673244.................................$16.95

Michael Brecker
00673237.................................$18.95

Michael Brecker Collection
00672429.................................$17.95

**The Brecker Brothers...
And All Their Jazz**
00672351.................................$19.95

Best of the Brecker Brothers
00672447.................................$19.95

Benny Carter Plays Standards
00672315.................................$22.95

Benny Carter Collection
00672314.................................$22.95

James Carter Collection
00672394.................................$19.95

John Coltrane – Giant Steps
00672349.................................$19.95

John Coltrane Solos
00673233.................................$22.95

Paul Desmond Collection
00672328.................................$19.95

Paul Desmond Plays Standards
00672454.................................$19.95

Stan Getz
00699375.................................$16.95

Stan Getz – Bossa Novas
00672377.................................$17.95

Great Tenor Sax Solos
00673254.................................$18.95

**Joe Henderson – Selections from
"Lush Life" & "So Near So Far"**
00673252.................................$19.95

Best of Joe Henderson
00672330.................................$22.95

Jazz Master Classics for Tenor Sax
00672350.................................$18.95

Best Of Kenny G
00673239.................................$19.95

Kenny G – Breathless
00673229.................................$19.95

Kenny G – Classics in the Key of G
00672462.................................$19.95

Kenny G – The Moment
00672373.................................$19.95

Joe Lovano Collection
00672326.................................$19.95

James Moody Collection – Sax and Flute
00672372.................................$19.95

The Frank Morgan Collection
00672416.................................$19.95

The Art Pepper Collection
00672301.................................$19.95

Sonny Rollins Collection
00672444.................................$19.95

David Sanborn Collection
00675000.................................$14.95

The Lew Tabackin Collection
00672455.................................$19.95

Stanley Turrentine Collection
00672334.................................$19.95

Ernie Watts Saxophone Collection
00673256.................................$18.95

1100